P9-ANY-160

SWAHILI
PHRASE BOOK
for Travelers in Eastern and Southern Africa

Compiled by
THEOPOLIS L. GILMORE
and
SHADRACK O. KWASA

HIPPOCRENE BOOKS
New York

Hippocrene paperback edition, 1991

Copyright © 1991, 1963

All rights reserved.

For information, contact:
HIPPOCRENE BOOKS, INC.
171 Madison Ave.
New York, N.Y. 10016

ISBN 0-87052-970-6

FOREWORD

ON THE CONTINENT OF AFRICA today approximately twenty million people speak Kiswahili, popularly known as Swahili. Spoken in the Eastern, Central, and Southern regions of the continent, it is rapidly expanding to the West and to the North.

This book will not help you to speak fluent Swahili, but the student or traveler will find it a practical guide to simple communication in the language. The pronunciation key is written in easily understood phonetic syllables to help the English speaker approximate the correct Swahili sound and diction.

Carefully selected English phrases most needed by visitors are given first, followed by the Swahili translations, with the phonetic key placed immediately after for quick, accurate pronunciation. The syllable which bears the stress or accent of the word is *italicized*.

Don't be timid. Use these phrases freely. They will serve your needs and make friends for you too, as you travel on the bright continent.

THEOPOLIS L. GILMORE
SHADRACK O. KWASA

iii

MAJOR SWAHILI-SPEAKING COUNTRIES AND THEIR CAPITALS

ANGOLA . . . . *Loanda*

BOTSWANA . . . . *Gaberones*

REPUBLIC OF BURUNDI . . . . *Bujumbura*

ZAIRE . . . . *Kinshasa*

ETHIOPIA . . . . *Addis Ababa*

KENYA . . . . *Nairobi*

MALAWI . . . . *Zomba*

MOZAMBIQUE . . . . *Lourenco Marques*

RHODESIA . . . . *Salisbury*

RWANDA . . . . *Kigali*

SOUTH AFRICA . . . . *Pretoria*

TANZANIA . . . . *Dar es Salaam*

UGANDA . . . . *Kampala*

ZAMBIA . . . . *Lusaka*

CONTENTS

GUIDE TO PRONUNCIATION

VOWELS

A = a as in mama
E = (has two sounds) ai as in pail and e as in
    get or let
I = ee as in feel
O = o as in bold or old
U = u as in rude or the oo as in fool

The vowels are represented in the phonetic key as:
ah, eh, ee, and oh.

CONSONANTS

The consonants in Swahili are the same as in English with the exception of the ones listed below:

C does not occur independently in Swahili but it does occur as ch and is equivalent to the ch sound as in cheap, chow, chew, etc.

D as in English except that Swahili has dh.

Dh is similar to the th sound in English as in this, that, therefore.

G is always hard, as in guard; it is never soft like the g as in George.

Gh = a guttural sounding g, familiar to German or Dutch. The correct sound is obtained by pronouncing the g with the mouth wide open; similar to the English word gobble.

H is never silent but is always a full consonant as the h in house.

Mb. Whenever M precedes the letter B in Swahili the M becomes nasal and practically silent.

M quite often stands for mu, and in such cases it is pronounced with a partially suppressed u sound before it. In some words, such as mtu, where the m bears the stress or accent of the word, it has a soft, semivowel sound, similar to um like humming. Where the letter M appears before any consonant except W, it must have this sound. Whenever this syllabic M occurs in the text, a stress mark is placed immediately above it.

M=m as in lu*mber* when it begins a word and is immediately followed by a consonant. It should be hummed with the mouth closed. It often has a syllabic mark over it in the text, especially in words like m̄tu (m̄-too), where it receives the stress of the word.

N. The n sound has several variations in Swahili.

N=n as in hunter without the "hu" when it begins a word and is immediately followed by a consonant. It should be hummed with the tongue against the teeth and the mouth open. It often has a syllabic mark over it, especially when it receives the stress in the word such as in n̄ne (n̄-neh).

Nd = the nd as in a*nd*, e*nd*, or ca*nd*y.

Ng' = the ng as in lo*ng*, wro*ng*, or so*ng*.

Ng = the ng as in *Congo*, co*ng*regate, or co*ng*ress.

Ny is a difficult sound for English speakers because there is no direct equivalent to it in English. The N is nasal with the stress on the Y sound although both N and Y are spoken almost simultaneously.

Q. There is no Q in the Swahili alphabet but whenever the letter K precedes the letter W as in Kwanza, the result is a Qu sound in English, similar to quaint or queer.

Th = the th as in thin or thick.

Whenever two vowels appear together at the end of a word, they often sound as one syllable (dipthong); but in actuality they are two distinct syllables with the stress on the first. For example: Kufaa (koo-f*a*h).

As in English, there is a difference in the tonal pitch of the voice when asking a question as compared with making a statement. In asking a question the pitch of the voice rises, usually on the next to last syllable of the last word in the sentence; the syllable which also bears the accent. The pitch does not fade as when making a statement but is sustained.

GENDER

All Swahili nouns are neuter with the exception of those which refer to living beings. Whenever a distinction of sex is necessary then the adjectives for male or female must be used.

mwanamume = male or man
(mwah-nah-*moo*-meh)
mwanamke = woman
(mwah-*nah*-mkeh)

SWAHILI NOUNS

Swahili nouns are divided into classes. Eight are important. Singular and plural are indicated by their prefixes.

Class 1	*Prefix*	*Singular*	*Plural*
		M	WA

This class includes all living beings or things and begins with m-, mu-, or mw-, in the singular and changes to wa-, in the plural.

*m*toto, child   *wa*toto, children

Class II		M	MI

Those nouns beginning with m-, mu-, or mw-, but not pertaining to living beings. The plural changes to mi-.

*m*ti, tree   *mi*ti, trees

Class III		N	N

Those nouns which do not change to form the plural.

*n*dizi, banana   *n*dizi, bananas
*n*yumba, house   *n*yumba, houses

Class IV		KI	VI

Nouns of this class begin with ki-, before a consonant and ch-, before a vowel. The plural is made by changing ki- to vi- and ch- to vy-.

*ki*tu, thing	*vi*tu, things
*ch*uo, school	*vy*uo, schools

Class V   MA

These nouns are made plural by the prefix ma-. As a rule, things that are usually in pairs belong to this class as do most liquids and fruit etc.

jicho, eye	*ma*cho, eyes
sikio, ear	*ma*sikio, ears

Class VI   U

Those nouns which begin with U- in the singular and change into ny- before a vowel or n- before a consonant to form the plural. Abstract nouns such as great*ness* or good*ness* also fall into this class.

For example: kubwa, large   *U*kubwa, largeness

Class VII   PA

The PA class denotes locations, as in, on, at, and by. Known as the locative case, it is formed by adding the suffix in- to any noun, singular or plural.

mto, river   mto*ni*, by the river

Class VIII   KU

This class embraces the infinitives of the verbs used as nouns (substantives).

*Ku*kaa, to sit, sitting
*Ku*fa, to die, dying

This is equal to the -ing in English.

ADJECTIVES

In Swahili, adjectives are generally made to agree with the noun by adding to them the prefixes proper to the class of the noun. For example: The stem -ema, good: The stem -dogo, small.

*m*tu *mw*ema, a good man   *k*itabu *k*idogo, a small book
*w*atu *we*ma, good men   *v*itabu *v*idogo, small books

CARDINAL NUMBERS

One	moja (*moh*-jah)
Two	mbili (*mbee*-lee)
Three	tatu (*tah*-too)
Four	nne (*n*-neh)
Five	tano (*tah*-noh)
Six	sita (*see*-tah)
Seven	saba (*sah*-bah)
Eight	nane (*nah*-neh)
Nine	tisa (*tee*-sah) or kenda (*keh*-ndah)
Ten	kumi (*koo*-mee)
Eleven	kumi na moja (*koo*-mee nah *moh*-jah)
Twenty	ishirini (ee-shee-*ree*-nee)
Twenty-one	ishirini na moja (ee-shee-*ree*-nee nah *moh*-jah)
Thirty	thelathini (theh-lah-*thee*-nee)
Thirty-one	thelathini na moja (theh-lah-*thee*-nee nah *moh*-jah)
Forty	arobaini (ah-roh-bah-*ee*-nee)
Fifty	hamsini (hah-*msee*-nee)
Sixty	sitini (see-*tee*-nee)
Seventy	sabwini (sah-*bwee*-nee)
Eighty	themanini (theh-mah-*nee*-nee)
Ninety	tisaini (tee-sah-*ee*-nee)
One hundred	mia moja (*mee*-ah *moh*-jah)
One thousand	elfu moja (*ehl*-foo *moh*-jah)
One million	millioni moja (mee-lee-*oh*-nee *moh*-jah)

ORDINAL NUMBERS

First	ya kwanza (yah *kwah*-nzah)
Second	ya pili (yah *pee*-lee)
Third	ya tatu (yah-*tah*-too)
Fourth	ya nne (yah *n*-neh)
Fifth	ya tano (yah-*tah*-noh)
Sixth	ya sita (yah *see*-tah)
Seventh	ya saba yah *sah*-bah)
Eighth	ya nane (yah nah-neh)
Ninth	ya tisa (yah *tee*-sah)
	ya kenda (yah *keh*-ndah)
Tenth	ya kumi (yah *koo*-mee)
Fifteenth	ya kumi na tano
	(yah *koo*-mee nah *tah*-noh)
Twentieth	ya ishirini (yah ee-shee-*ree*-nee)
Twenty-fifth	ya ishirini na tano
	(yah ee-shee-*ree*-nee nah *tah*-noh)

SIGNS TO WATCH

IN TOWN

No smoking
>   Hakuna kuvuta sigara
>   (hah-*koo*-nah koo-*voo* tah see-*gah*-rah)

Danger
>   Hatari (hah-*tah*-ree)

Toilet
>   Choo (choo)

Men
>   Wanaume (wah-nah-*oo*-meh)

Women
>   Wanawake (wah-nah-*wah*-keh)

Occupied
>   Hakuna nafasi (hah-*koo*-nah nah-*fah*-see)

Free
>   Bure (boo-reh)

No admittance
>   Hakuna kuingia
>   (hah-*koo*-nah koo-ee-*ngee-ah*)

Attention
>   Sikia (See-kee-ah)

Entrance
>   Mlango (*m-lah*-ngoh)

Exit
>   Nje (nj*eh*)

Open
>   Fungua (foo-*ngoo*-ah)

Closed
>   Funga (*foo*-ngah)

Quiet
>   Nyamaza (nyah-*mah*-zah)

Hospital
      Hospitali (hoh-spee-*tah*-lee)

School
      Shule (*shoo*-leh)

Information
      Maelezo (mah-eh-*leh*-zoh)

Caution
      Jihadhari (jee-hah-*thah*-ree)

Bus stop
      Kituo cha basi
      (kee-*too*-oh chah *bah*-see)

No spitting
      Hakuna kutema mate
      (hah-*koo*-nah koo-teh-mah *mah*-teh)

Keep off the grass
      Usitembee majanini
      (oo-see-teh-mbeh mah-jah-*nee*-nee)

Wet paint
      Rangi majimaji
      (*rah*-ngee *mah*-jee-*mah*-jee)

No fishing
      Hakuna kuvua samaki
      (hah-*koo*-nah koo-*voo*-ah sah-*mah*-kee)

No hunting
      Hakuna kuwinda
      (hah-*koo*-nah koo-*wee*-ndah)

Post no bills
      Usitume noti kwa posta
      (oo-see-*too*-mah *noh*-tee kwah *poh*-stah)

Office
      Afisi (ah-*fee*-see)

Manager
      Bwana mkubwa (bwah-nah *mkoo*-bwah)

Cashier
      Mtoa fedha (*mtoh*-ah *feh*-thah)

ROAD SIGNS

No thoroughfare
Hakuna m̄pisho (hah-*koo*-nah m̄*pee*-shoh)

Keep right
Kuwa <u>kulia</u> (koo-wah koo-*lee*-ah)

Keep left
Kuwa <u>kushoto</u> (koo-wah koo-*shoh*-toh)

No parking
Hakuna kusimama
(hah-*koo*-nah koo-see-*mah*-mah)

Detour
M̄kato (m̄*kah*-toh)

Intersection
Njia zapitana (*njee*-ah zah-pee-*tah*-nah)

Crossroads
Njia zapitana (*njee*-ah zah-pee-*tah*-nah)

Sharp curve
Kona ya hatari (*koh*-nah yah hah-*tah*-ree)

Main highway
Njia kubwa (njee-ah *koo*-bwah)

Slippery when wet
Huteleza (hoo-teh-*leh*-zah)

Narrow
Mpana (*mpah*-nah)

Railway crossing
Hupita reli (hoo-*pee*-tah *reh*-lee)

Animal crossing
Mpito wa wanyama
(*mpee*-toh wah wah-*nyah*-mah)

Stop
Simama (see-*mah*-mah)

One way
Njia moja (*njee*-ah *moh*-jah)

Low bridge
Daraja fupi (dah-*rah*-jah *foo*-pee)

Weight limit

Uzito wa chini (oo-*zee*-toh wah *chee*-nee)

Slow

Pole pole (*poh*-leh *poh*-leh)

Hill

Mlima (*mlee*-mah)

Speed limit

Mwendo wa chini (*mweh*-ndoh wah *chee*-nee)

BASIC PHRASES

Hello
> Jambo (*jah*-mboh)

Hello (in reply)
> Jambo (*jah*-mboh)

Yes
> Ndiyo (*ndee*-yoh)

No
> La (*lah*)

Thank you
> Asante (ah-*sah*-nteh)

You are welcome
> Si kitu (see *kee*-too)

→ *Excuse me*
> Nisemehe (nee-seh-*meh*-heh)

Please
> Tafadhali (tah-fah-*thah*-lee)

All right
> Si neno (see *neh*-noh)

How much?
> Ngapi? (*ngah*-pee)

— *Where?*
> Wapi? (*wah*-pee)

— *When?*
> Lini? (*lee*-nee)

I do not understand.
> Sielewi. (see-eh-*leh*-wee)

I understand.
> Naelewa. (nah-eh-*leh*-wah)

Speak slowly.
> Sema pole pole. (*seh*-mah *poh*-leh *poh*-leh)

Please repeat.
> Tafadhali sema tena.
> (tah-fah-*thah*-lee *seh*-mah *teh*-nah)

11

→ *How are you?*
> Habari yako? (hah-bah-ree *yah*-koh)

Very well (thank you).
> Njema. (*njeh*-mah)

Pleased to meet you.
> Nimefurahi sana kwa kukuona.
> (nee-meh-foo-*rah*-hee sah-nah kwah
> koo-koo-*oh*-nah)

→ *How long will it take?*
> Itachukua muda gani?
> (ee-tah-choo-*koo*-ah moo-dah *gah*-nee)

→ *How far?*
> Ni umbali gani? (nee oo-*mbah*-lee *gah*-nee)

How many?
> Vingapi? (vee-*ngah*-pee)

I am lost.
> Nimepotea. (nee-meh-poh-*teh*-ah)

My name is ....
> Jina langu .... (jee-nah *lah*-ngoo............)

I have a little money.
> Nina pesa kidogo.
> (nee-nah *peh*-sah kee-*doh*-goh)

Goodbye.
> Kwaheri. (kwah-*heh*-ree)

Goodbye (in reply).
> Kwaheri ya kuonana.
> (kwah-*heh*-ree yah koo-oh-*nah*-nah)

ARRIVAL

Here is my passport.
> Pasipoti yangu ni hii.
> (pah-see-*poh*-tee *yah*-ngoo nee h*ee*)

Is it in order?
> Ni sawa sawa? (nee sah-wah *sah*-wah)

Landing card
> Cheti changu ni hii
> (cheh-tee *chah*-ngoo nee h*ee*)

This is my vaccination certificate.
> Hiki ndicho cheti changu cha mchanjo.
> (*hee*-kee *ndee*-choh cheh-tee *chah*-ngoo chah
> m-*chah*-njoh)

These are my bags.
> Hii ndiyo mizigo yangu.
> (h*ee* *ndee*-yoh mee-zee-goh *yah*-ngoo)

That is my bag.
> Huu ni mzigo wangu.
> (hoo nee *mzee*-goh *wah*-ngoo)

Here are my claim checks.
> Cheki za madai yangu ni hizi.
> (*cheh*-kee zah mah-*dah*-ee yah-ngoo nee
> *hee*-zee)

My name is John Smith.
> Jina langu John Smith.
> (jee-nah *lah*-ngoo John Smith)

What is your name?
> Jina lako nani? (jee-nah *lah*-koh *nah*-nee)

I have nothing to declare.
> Sina kitu cha kutangaza.
> (see-nah *kee*-too chah koo-tah-*ngah*-zah)

May I close my bags now?
> Naweza kufunga mizigo yangu sasa?
> (nah-weh-zah koo-*foo*-ngah mee-*zee*-goh
> yah-ngoo *sah*-sah)

Where can I change money?
> Naweza kugeuza pesa wapi?
> (nah-weh-zah koo-*geh*-oozah *peh*-sah *wah*-pee)

What is the rate for dollars?
> Dola moja ni pesa ngapi?
> (doh-lah *moh*-jah nee *peh*-sah *ngah*-pee)

Please change this money.
> Tafadhali wageza pesa hii.
> (tah-fah-*thah*-lee wah-*geh*-oozah peh-sah h*ee*)

Where is the men's room?
> Nina haja. Wapi kichumba cha wanaume?
> (nee-nah *hah*-jah. wah-pee kee-*choo*-mbah chah
> wah-nah-*oo*-meh)

Over there.
> Kule. (*koo*-leh)

Where is the ladies' room?
> Nina haja. Wapi kichumba cha wanawake?
> (nee-nah *hah*-jah. wah-pee kee-*choo*-mbah chah
> wah-nah-*wah*-keh)

Here.
> Hapa. (*hah*-pah)

I can carry my own bags, thank you.
> Naweza kuchukua mizigo yangu, asante.
> (nah-*weh*-zah koo-choo-koo-ah mee-*zee*-goh
> yah-ngoo, ah-*sah*-nteh)

Please take my bags to a taxi.
> Tafadhali peleka mizigo yangu kwa teksi.
> (tah-fah-*thah*-lee peh-leh-kah mee-*zee*-goh
> yahn-goo kwah *tehk*-see)

Bring the bags here.
> Lete mizigo hapa.
> (leh-teh mee-*zee*-goh *hah*-pah)

Where is a good hotel?
> Hoteli ñzuri iko wapi?
> (hoh-*teh*-leeñ -*zoo*-ree ee-koh *wah*-pee)

How are the prices?
> Bei ni mamna gani?
> (*beh*-ee nee *nah*-mnah *gah*-nee)

How much is the fare?
> Bei ya kwenda kwa hoteli ni nini?
> (*Beh*-ee yah *kweh*-ndah kwah hoh-*teh*-lee
> nee *nee*-nee)

Take me there.
> Unipeleka huko.
> (oo-nee-peh-*leh*-kah *hoo*-koh)

Take me to the .... hotel.
> Nipeleke .... hoteli.
> (nee-peh-*leh*-keh........... hoh-*teh*-lee)

Very good. Thank you.
> Vizuri sana. Asante.
> (vee-*zoo*-ree *sah*-nah. Ah-*sah*-nteh)

AT THE HOTEL

Do you have a reservation for Mr. Smith?
> Uliweka chumba kwa Bwana Smith?
> (oo-lee-*weh*-kah *choo*-mbah kwah bwah-nah
> Smith)

I am Mr. Smith.
> Bwana Smith ni mimi.
> (bwah-nah Smith ni *mee*-mee)

Do you have a vacancy?
> Una nafasi? (*oo*-nah nah-*fah*-see)

Do you have a room with a bath?
> Una chumba chenye kiogeo?
> (oo-nah *choo*-mbah cheh-nyeh kee-oh-*geh*-oh)

Do you have a room without a bath?
> Una chumba bila kiogeo?
> (oo-nah *choo*-mbah bee-lah kee-oh-*geh*-oh)

How much per day?
> Ni bei gani kwa siku?
> (nee *beh*-ee *gah*-nee kwah *see*-koo)

I shall stay for four days.
> Nitakaa siku ñne
> (nee-tah-k*a*h see-koo *n*-neh)

How much per week?
> Ni bei gani kwa juma?
> (nee *beh*-ee *gah*-nee kwah *joo*-mah)

For one person.
> Kwa mtu mmoja. (kwah *m*-too *moh*-jah)

For two.
> Kwa watu wawili.
> (kwah *wah*-too wah-*wee*-lee)

Are the meals included?
> Pamoja na chakula?
> (pah-*moh*-jah nah chah-*koo*-lah)

Is breakfast included?
> Chakula asabuhi pia?
> (chah-*koo*-lah ah-sah-*boo*-hee *pee*-ah)

Is there a shower?
>Iko nyumba ya kuoga?
>(ee-koh *nyoo*-mbah yah koo-*oh*-gah)

This room is too hot.
>Chumba hiki ina joto zaidi
>(choo-mbah *hee*-kee ee-nah-*joh*-toh
>zah-*ee*-dee)

This room is too dark.
>Chumba hiki kina giza zaidi.
>(choo-mbah *hee*-kee kee-nah *gee*-zah
>zah-*ee*-dee)

This room is too sunny.
>Chumba hiki kina jua zaidi.
>(choo-mbah *hee*-kee kee-nah *joo*-ah
>zah-*ee*-dee)

This room is too noisy.
>Chumba hiki kina kelele zaidi.
>(choo-mbah *hee*-kee kee-nah keh-*leh*-leh
>zah-*ee*-dee)

This room is too large.
>Chumba hiki ni kipana zaidi.
>(choo-mbah *hee*-kee nee kee-*pah*-nah
>zah-*ee*-dee)

This room is too small.
>Chumba hiki ni kidogo zaidi.
>(choo-mbah *hee*-kee nee kee-*doh*-goh
>zah-*ee*-dee)

Do you have a better room?
>Una chumba kizuri zaidi?
>(oo-nah *choo*-mbah kee-*zoo*-ree zah-*ee*-dee)

Do you have a room with a view?
>Una chumba chenye upeo wa macho?
>(oo-nah *choo*-mbah cheh-nyeh oo-*peh*-oh wah
>*mah*-choh)

Do you have a less expensive room?
>Una chumba rahisi kidogo?
>(*oo*-nah choo-mbah rah-*hee*-see kee-*doh*-goh)

This room is satisfactory.
> Chumba hiki chanitosha.
> (choo-mbah *hee*-kee chah-nee-*toh*-shah)

Do you have a fan?
> Una kipepeo? (*oo*-nah kee-peh-*peh*-oh)

SERVICE

Please bring my breakfast to my room.
> Tafadhali lete chai yangu ya asabuhi chum-
> bani.
> (tah-fah-*thah*-lee *leh*-teh chah-ee *yah*-ngoo
> yah ah-sah-*boo*-hee choo-*mbah*-nee)

Where is the telephone?
> Wapi telephoni? (*wah*-pee teh-leh-*phoh*-nee)

Do you have a match?
> Una kiberiti? (*oo*-nah kee-beh-*ree*-tee)

Where is the bathroom?
> Wapi chumba cha kuoga?
> (wah-pee *choo*-mbah chah koo-*oh*-gah)

Please send the waiter.
> Tafadhali tuma m̄tumishi.
> (tah-fah-*thah*-lee too-mah m̄-too-*mee*-shee)

Please send the chambermaid.
> Tafadhali tuma mtumishi.

Please take these clothes to the laundry.
> Tafadhali peleka nguo hizi kwa dobi.
> (tah-fah-*thah*-lee peh-*leh*-kah *ngoo*-oh hee-zee
> kwah doh-bee)

Please have these clothes cleaned.
> Tafadhali tuma nguo hizi kwa dobi.
> (tah-fah-*thah*-lee too-mah *ngoo*-oh *hee*-zee
> kwoh *doh*-bee)

I want them pressed only.
> Nataka zipigwe pasi tu.
> (nah-*tah*-kah zee-*pee*-gweh pah-see too)

I need them at once.
>Nazitaka maramoja.
>(nah-zee-*tah*-kah mah-rah-*moh*-jah)

I want these shoes shined.
>Nataka viatu hivi vipigwe rangi
>(nah-tah-kah vee-*ah*-too hee-vee vee-*pee*-gweh *rah*-ngee)

What time is lunch?
>Chakula cha adhuhuri ni saa ngapi?
>(chah-*koo*-lah chah ah-thoo-*hoo*-ree nee *sah ngah*-pee)

What time is dinner?
>Chakula cha jioni ni saa ngapi?
>(chah-*koo*-lah chah jee-*oh*-nee nee *sah ngah*-pee)

Please mail these for me.
>Tafadhali nitumie hii kwa posta.
>(tah-fah-*thah*-lee nee-too-*mee*-eh hee kwah *poh*-stah)

Is there any mail for me?
>Iko barua yangu?
>(ee-koh bah-*roo*-ah *yah*-ngoo)

I need an interpreter.
>Nataka m̄kalimani.
>(*nah*-tah-kah m̄-kah-lee-*mah*-nee)

I need a guide.
>Nataka mwongozi.
>(nah-*tah*-kah mwo-*ngoh*-zee)

I need an English speaking guide.
>Nataka kiongozi asemaye kiingereza.
>(nah-*tah*-kah kee-oh-*ngoh*-zee ah-seh-*mah*-yah kee-ee-ngeh-*reh*-zah)

I need some writing paper.
>Nataka karatasi.
>(nah-*tah*-kah kah-rah-*tah*-see)

I need an envelope.
Nataka bahasha. (nah-*tah*-kah bah-*hah*-shah)

I need some stamps.
Nataka sitampu. (nah-*tah*-kah see-*tah*-mpoo)

Here is my key.
Ufunguo wangu ni huu.
(oo-foo-*ngoo*-oh *wah*-ngoo nee hoo)

My key please.
Nataka ufunguo wangu.
(nah-*tah*-kah oo-foo-*ngoo*-oh *wah*-ngoo)

Please bring towels.
Tafadhali lete taulo.
(tah-fah-*thah*-lee leh-teh tah-*oo*-loh)

Bring soap.
Lete sabuni.
(*leh*-teh sah-*boo*-nee)

The water is too cold.
Maji ni baridi sana.
(mah-jee nee bah-*ree*-dee *sah*-nah)

I need some cigarettes.
Nataka sigara. (nah-*tah*-kah see-*gah*-rah)

I am ready to leave.
Mimi tayari kutoka.
(mee-mee tah-*yah*-ree koo-*toh*-kah)

May I come in?
Hodi? (*hoh*-dee)

Enter.
Karibu. (kah-*ree*-boo)

Who is there?
Ni nani huko? (nee *nah*-nee *hoo*-koh)

Are there any telegrams or phone calls for me?
Iko simu yoyote kwangu?
(ee-koh *see*-moo yoh-*yoh*-teh *kwah*-ngoo)

There is no mail.
Hakuna mabaruwa.
(hah-*koo*-nah mah-bah-*roo*-wah)

Nobody called for you.

Mtu hakukuita. (m̄-too hah-koo-koo-*ee*-tah)

I need them soon.

Naitaka upesi. (nah-ee-*tah*-kah oo-*peh*-see)

Someone wants to see you.

M̄tu ataka kukuona.

(*m*-too ah-*tah*-kah koo-koo-*oh* nah)

I must go.

Lazima nienda. (lah-*zee*-mah nee-*eh*-ndah)

We must go.

Lazima twende. (lah-*zee*-mah *tweh*-ndeh)

Where is the American Consulate?

Konsuleti ya Amerika iko wapi?

(koh-nsoo-*leh*-tee yah Ah-meh-*ree*-kah ee-koh *wah*-pee)

What is my bill?

Deni yangu ni nini?

(deh-nee *yah*-ngoo nee *nee*-nee)

Is everything included?

Kila kitu kiko ndani?

(kee-lah *kee*-too kee-koh *ndah*-nee)

TRAVEL

BY PLANE

I wish to go to the airport.
> Nataka kwenda uwanja wandege.
> (nah-*tah*-kah kweh-ndah oo-*wah*-njah
> wah-*ndeh*-geh)

I wish to fly to Kampala.
> Nataka kwenda Kampala.
> (nah-*tah*-kah kweh-ndah Kah-*mpah*-lah)

I want a one-way ticket.
> Nataka tikiti ya kwenda tu.
> (nah-*tah*-kah tee-*kee*-tee yah *kweh*-ndah too)

I want a round-trip ticket.
> Nataka tikiti ya kwenda na kurudi.
> (nah-*tah*-kah tee-*kee*-tee yah kweh-ndah nah
> koo-*roo*-dee)

What is the price?
> Ni bei gani? (nee *beh*-ee *gah*-nee)

Here is my baggage.
> Mizigo yangu ni hii.
> (mee-zee-goh *yah*-ngoo nee hee)

How much do I have to pay for excess baggage?
> Nilipe nini kwa mizigo zaidi?
> (nee-*lee*-peh nee-nee kwah mee-*zee*-goh
> zah-*ee*-dee)

What time does my flight leave?
> Ndege huruka saa ngapi?
> (*ndeh*-geh hoo-*roo*-kah sah *ngah*-pee)

Can I purchase insurance?
> Naweza kununua suransi?
> (nah-*weh*-zah koo-noo-*noo*-ah soo-*rah*-nsee)

I wish to cancel my reservation.
> Nataka kukomesha maagizo yangu.
> (nah-tah-kah koo-koh-*meh*-shah
> mah-ah-*gee*-zoh *yah*-ngoo)

22

What is my seat number?

Kiti changu ni nambari gani?

(kee-tee *chah*-ngoo nee nah-*mbah*-ree *gah*-nee)

I feel sick.

Nasikia vibaya. (nah-see-*kee*-ah vee-*bah*-yah)

I want some coffee.

Nataka kahawa. (nah-*tah*-kah kah-*hah*-wah)

I feel better.

Naona nafuu. (nah-*oh*-nah nah-foo)

Where are we now?

Tuko wapi sasa? (too-koh *wah*-pee *sah*-sah)

How far is the next airport?

Kituo chetu cha mbele ki wapi?

(kee-too-oh *cheh*-too chah *mbeh*-leh kee *wah*-pee)

How long will we stay here?

Tutakaa huko muda gani?

(too-tah-*kah* hoo-koh *moo*-dah *gah*-nee)

Where can I get my baggage?

Naweza kupata mizigo yangu wapi?

(nah-weh-zah koo-*pah*-tah mee-*zee*-goh yah-ngoo *wah*-pee)

BY TRAIN

Where is the railroad station?

Stesheni la gari liko wapi?

(steh-*sheh*-nee lah *gah*-ree lee-koh *wah*-pee)

I want a ticket to Nairobi.

Nataka tikiti ya Nairobi.

(nah-tah-kah tee-*kee*-tee yah Nah-ee-*roh*-bee)

One-way or round-trip?

Njia moja au kwenda na kurudi?

(*njee*-ah *moh*-jah ah-oo *kweh*-ndah nah koo-*roo*-dee)

What is the price for children?

Bei kwa watoto ni nini?

(*beh*-ee kwah wah-*toh*-toh nee *nee*-nee)

Please give me a timetable.
>Tafadhali nipe muhtahsari.
>(tah-fah-*thah*-lee nee-peh mooh-tah-*sah*-ree)

Will the train be on time?
>Gari litafika mapema?
>(gah-ree lee-tah-*fee*-kah mah-*peh*-mah)

Is it an express train?
>Ni gari la haraka?
>(nee *gah*-ree lah hah-*rah*-kah)

How much do the berths cost?
>Vijumba ni vya bei gani?
>(vee-*joo*-mbah nee vyah *beh*-ee *gah*-nee)

First class
>Vya kwanza (vyah *kwah*-nzah)

Second class
>Vya pili (vyah *pee*-lee)

Third class
>Vya tatu (vyah *tah*-too)

Here is my ticket.
>Tikiti yangu ni hii.
>(tee-kee-tee *yah*-ngoo nee h*ee*)

These are my bags.
>Hii ni mizigo yangu.
>(h*ee* nee mee-*zee*-goh *yah*-ngoo)

Please put my bags on the train.
>Tafadhali tia mizigo yangu garini.
>(tah-fah-*thah*-lee tee-ah mee-*zee*-goh yah-ngoo gah-*ree*-nee)

Is this seat occupied?
>Kiti hiki kimechukuliwa?
>(kee-tee *hee*-kee kee-meh-choo-koo-*lee*-wah)

That is my seat.
>Hiki ni kiti changu.
>(*hee*-kee nee *kee*-tee *chah*-ngoo)

May I sit here?
>Nikae hapa? (nee-*kah*-eh *hah*-pah)

Please open the window.
> Tafadhali fungua dirisha.
> (tah-fah-*thah*-lee foo-*ngoo*-ah dee-*ree*-shah)

Please close the window.
> Tafadhali funga dirisha.
> (tah-fah-*thah*-lee *foo*-ngah dee-*ree*-shah)

My coach number is................
> Nambari ya kichumba changu ni................
> (nah-*mbah*-ree yah-kee-*choo*-mbah chah-ngoo
> nee............)

Are you the porter?
> Wewe ndiwe mchukuzi?
> (weh-weh *ndee*-weh mchoo-*koo*-zee)

Please make my berth up now.
> Tafadhali nitandikie kitanda sasa.
> (tah-fah-*thah*-lee nee-tah-ndee-*kee*-eh
> kee-tah-ndah *sah*-sah)

Please call me at seven.
> Tafadhali niite saa moja.
> (tah-fah-*thah*-lee nee-*ee*-teh s*a*h moh-jah)

Is there a dining car?
> Kuna kichumba cha kulia?
> (koo-nah kee-*choo*-mbah chah koo-*lee*-ah)

What time are meals served?
> Vyakula viko tayari saa ngapi?
> (vyah-*koo*-lah vee-koh tah-*yah*-ree s*a*h
> *ngah*-pee)

May I smoke?
> Naweza kuvuta sigara?
> (nah-*weh*-zah koo-*voo*-tah see-*gah*-rah)

What time does the train arrive?
> Gari lafika saa ngapi?
> (gah-ree lah-*fee*-kah s*a*h ngah-pee)

Is the train late?
> Gari limechelewa?
> (*gah*-ree lee-meh-cheh-*leh*-wah)

Why is the train stopping?
>Kwa nini gari linasimama?
>(kwah *nee*-nee *gah*-ree lee-nah-see-*mah*-mah)

Is something wrong?
>Kuna habari? (*koo*-nah hah-*bah*-ree)

How long does the train stop in Nakuru?
>Gari lasimama Nakuru kwa muda gani?
>(*gah*-ree lah-see-*mah*-mah nah-*koo*-roo kwah
>moo-dah *gah*-nee)

Where is the baggage room?
>Nyumba ya mizigo iko wapi?
>(*nyoo*-mbah yah mee-*zee*-goh ee-koh *wah*-pee)

Here are my baggage checks.
>Cheki ya mizigo yangu ni hizi.
>(*cheh*-kee yah mee-*zee*-goh yah-ngoo nee
>*hee*-zee)

Please get me a taxi.
>Tafadhali nipatie teksi.
>(tah-fah-*thah*-lee nee-pah-*tee*-eh *tehk*-see)

Please put my baggage in a taxi.
>Tafadhali tia mizigo yangu ndani ya teksi.
>(tah-fah-*thah*-lee tee-ah mee-*zee*-goh yah-ngoo
>*ndah*-nee yah *tehk*-see)

How much is it for my baggage?
>Nauli gani kwa mizigo yangu?
>(nah-oo-lee *gah*-nee kwah mee-*zee*-goh
>*yah*-ngoo)

BY TAXI

Taxi!
>Teksi! (*tehk*-see)

What is the fare to Kaloleni?
>Ni bei gani mpaka Kaloleni?
>(nee beh-ee *gah*-nee *mpah*-kah
>kah-loh-*leh*-nee)

Do you have an hourly rate?
>Mna malipo kwa saa?
>(m̄-nah mah-*lee*-poh kwah saa)

Do you have a daily rate?
>Mna malipo kwa siku?
>(m̄-nah mah-*lee*-poh kwah *see*-koo)

Are you a guide?
>Wewe ni kiongozi?
>(*weh*-weh nee kee-oh-*ngoh*-zee)

Please show me the interesting sights.
>Tafadhali nionyeshe mahali pa kupendeza.
>tah-fah-*thah*-lee nee-oh-*nyeh*-sheh mah-*hah*-lee
>pah koo-peh-*ndeh*-zah)

Is it very far?
>Ni mbali sana? (nee *mbah*-lee *sah*-nah)

Take me to town.
>Nipeleke mjini. (nee-peh-*leh*-keh *mjee*-nee)

I wish to tour the city.
>Nataka kusafiria mjini.
>(nah-*tah*-kah koo-sah-fee-*ree*-ah *mjee*-nee)

Stop here.
>Simama hapa. (see-*mah*-mah *hah*-pah)

Stop at the next corner.
>Simama kwa punduko la mbele.
>(see-*mah*-mah kwah poo-*ndoo*-koh lah
>*mbeh*-leh)

Turn left.
>Geuka kushoto. (geh-*oo*-kah koo-*shoh*-toh)

Turn right.
>Geuka kulia. (geh-*oo*-kah koo-*lee*-ah)

What is that?
>Kile ni nini? (*kee*-leh nee *nee*-nee)

Who are these people?
>Watu wale ni nani?
>(*wah*-too wah-leh nee *nah*-nee)

What are they doing?
    Wanafanya nini? (wah-nah-*fah*-nyah *nee*-nee)

Keep driving. (proceed)
    Endelea. (eh-ndeh-*leh-ah*)

Please take me to a good restaurant.
    Tafadhali nipeleke mgawani m̄zuri.
    (tah-fah-*thah*-lee nee-peh-*leh*-keh
    mgah-*wah*-nee *mzoo*-ree)

Take me to the shopping district.
    Nipeleke kwenye maduka.
    (nee-peh-*leh*-keh kweh-nyeh mah-*doo*-kah)

Please wait for me.
    Tafadhali ningojee.
    (tah-fah-*thah*-lee nee-ngoh-jeh)

Is my baggage extra?
    M̄zigo wangu ni m̄zito zaidi?
    (mzee-goh *wah*-ngoo nee *mzee*-toh zah-*ee*-dee)

Can you pick me up later?
    Waweza kunichukua baadaye?
    (wah-*weh*-zah koo-nee-choo-*koo*-ah
    bah-ah-*dah*-yeh)

How much do I owe you?
    Nina deni yako ya nini?
    (*nee*-nah deh-nee *yah*-koh yah *nee*-nee)

Here is the amount we agreed upon.
    Hiki ndicho kiasi tulichokubaliana.
    (*hee*-kee ndee-choh kee-*ah*-see
    too-lee-choh-koo-bah-lee-*ah*-nah)

No, that is not right.
    La, Si sawa. (*lah*, see *sah*-wah)

The trip has been very pleasant.
    Safari imekuwa ya kupendeza sana.
    (sah-*fah*-ree ee-meh-*koo*-wah yah
    koo-peh-*ndeh*-zah sah-nah)

Here is something for your kindness.
Kitu kidogo hapa kwa hisani yako.
(*kee*-too kee-doh-goh *hah*-pah kwah
hee-*sah*-nee *yah*-koh)

TRAVEL BY BUS (local)

Where is the bus stop?
Kituo cha basi kiko wapi?
(kee-*too*-oh chah *bah*-see kee-koh *wah*-pee)

I wish to go to the shopping district.
Nataka kwenda kwenye maduka.
(nah-*tah*-kah kweh-ndah *kweh*-nyeh
mah-*doo*-kah)

How many stops is it from here?
Kuna vituo vingapi kutoka hapa?
(*koo*-nah vee-too-oh vee-*ngah*-pee koo-*toh*-kah
hah-pah)

Where do I pay the fare?
Nauli yangu nalipa wapi?
(nah-oo-lee *yah*-ngoo nah-*lee*-pah *wah*-pee)

What street is this?
Njia hii ni ipi?
(*njee*-ah hee nee *ee*-pee)

Do I get off here?
Natoka hapa ama je?
(nah-*toh*-kah hah-pah *ah*-mah *jeh*)

I wish to sit here.
Napenda kukaa hapa.
(nah-*peh*-ndah koo-k*ah* hah-pah)

TRAVEL BY BUS

Where is the station?
Kituo cha basi kiko wapi?
(kee-*too*-oh chah *bah*-see kee-koh *wah*-pee)

How much is a ticket to Kisumu?
    Tikiti ya Kisumu ni bei gani?
    (tee-*kee*-tee yah kee-*soo*-moo nee beh-ee
    gah-nee)

What time does the bus leave?
    Basi yatoka saa ngapi?
    (bah-see yah-*toh*-kah sah *ngah*-pee)

What time does the bus arrive?
    Basi yafika saa ngapi?
    (bah-see yah-*fee*-kah sah *ngah*-pee)

Will there be a rest-room stop?
    Kutakuwako nyumba ya kiburudisho?
    (koo-tah-koo-*wah*-koh *nyoo*-mbah yah
    kee-boo-roo-*dee*-shoh)

I have not eaten yet.
    Sijala bado. (see-*jah*-lah *bah*-doh)

Will we be able to eat?
    Tutaweza kula? (too-tah-*weh*-zah *koo*-lah)

Do I get off here?
    Natoka hapa ama je?
    (nah-*toh*-kah hah-pah *ah*-mah *jeh*)

Does this bus go to town?
    Basi hii yaenda mjini?
    (bah-see hee yah-*eh*-ndah *mjee*-nee)

What is the fare?
    Ni bei gani? (nee *beh*-ee *gah*-nee)

How far is it?
    Ni umbali gani? (nee oo-*mbah*-lee *gah*-nee)

Is this seat taken?
    Kiti hiki kimechukuliwa?
    (kee-tee *hee*-kee kee-meh-choo-koo-*lee*-wah)

May I smoke?
    Naweza kuvuta sigara?
    (nah-*weh*-zah koo-voo-tah see-*gah*-rah)

Must I change buses?
>Ni lazima nigeuze basi?
>(nee lah-*zee*-mah nee-geh-*oo*-zeh *bah*-see)

Please tell me where to get off.
>Tafadhali niambie wakati wa kutoka.
>(tah-fah-*thah*-lee nee-ah-*mbee*-eh wah-*kah*-tee
>wah koo-*toh*-kah)

Will we pass any interesting places?
>Tutapitia mahali popote maarufu?
>(too-tah-pee-*tee*-ah mah-hah-lee poh-*poh*-teh
>mah-ah-*roo*-foo)

TRAVEL BY PRIVATE AUTO

I need some gasoline.
>Nataka petroli. (nah-*tah*-kah peh-*troh*-lee)

I need some oil.
>Nataka oili. (nah-*tah*-kah oh-*ee*-lee)

Please change the oil.
>Tafadhali geuza oili.
>(tah-fah-*thah*-lee geh-*oo*-zah oh-*ee*-lee)

Please fill up my tank.
>Tafadhali jaza tanki yangu.
>(tah-fah-*thah*-lee jah-zah *tah*-nkee *yah*-ngoo)

Check the water.
>Angalia maji. (ah-ngah-*lee*-ah *mah*-jee)

I need air in the tires.
>Nataka pumsi ya gurudumu.
>(nah-tah-kah *poo*-msee yah goo-roo-*doo*-moo)

Do you have a road map?
>Una ramani ya njia?
>(oo-nah rah-*mah*-nee yah *njee*-ah)

How much?
>Ngapi? (*ngah*-pee)

How far is it to Kilimanjaro?
>Kilimanjaro ni umbali gani kutoka hapa?
>kee-lee-mah-*njah*-roh nee oo-mbah-lee
>*gah*-nee koo-*toh*-kah *hah*-pah)

Which is the best road to Kilimanjaro?
>Njia nzuri ya Kilimanjaro ni ipi?
>(njee-ah *nzoo*-ree yah Kee-lee-mah-*njah*-roh
>nee *ee*-pee)

Is it a good road?
>Ni njia nzuri? (nee *njee*-ah *nzoo*-ree)

I am lost.
>Nimepotea. (nee-meh-poh-*teh*-ah)

Do I go straight ahead?
>Niendelee mbele? (nee-eh-ndeh-leh *mbeh*-leh)

Do I turn left or right?
>Nigeuke kushoto ama kulia?
>(nee-geh-*oo*-keh koo-*shoh*-toh ah-mah
>koo-*lee*-ah)

Do I go across the bridge?
>Nipite daraja? (nee-*pee*-teh dah-*rah*-jah)

Is there a policeman nearby?
>Kuna polisi karibuni?
>(koo-nah poh-*lee*-see kah-ree-*boo*-nee)

SERVICE

I need a mechanic.
>Nataka mekanika.
>(nah-*tah*-kah meh-kah-*nee*-kah)

Is there a mechanic here?
>Kuna mekanika hapa?
>(*koo*-nah meh-kah-*nee*-kah *hah*-pah)

Where is there a garage?
>Garagi iko wapi? (gah-*rah*-gee ee-koh *wah*-pee)

Grease the car.
>Tia girisi. (*tee*-ah gee-*ree*-see)

The motor runs badly.
> Engini si sawa sawa.
> (eh-*ngee*-nee see sah-wah *sah*-wah)

The motor gets too hot.
> Engini ina moto sana.
> (eh-*ngee*-nee ee-nah *moh*-toh *sah*-nah)

The car will not start.
> Motokaa haianzi.
> (moh-toh-k*ah* hah-ee-*ah*-nzee)

My battery is dead.
> Batari yangu imelala.
> (bah-tah-ree *yah*-ngoo ee-meh-*lah*-lah)

Please examine it.
> Tafadhali ichungulie.
> (tah-fah-*thah*-lee ee-choo-ngoo-*lee*-eh)

What is the matter?
> Habari gani? (hah-bah-ree *gah*-nee)

Can you fix it?
> Waweza kuitengeneza?
> (wah-*weh*-zah koo-ee-teh-ngeh-*neh*-zah)

How long will it take to fix it?
> Itachukuwa muda gani kuitengeneza?
> (ee-tah-choo-*koo*-wah moo-dah *gah*-nee
> koo-ee-teh-ngeh-*neh*-zah)

Can you fix it temporarily?
> Waweza kuitengeneza kwa siku kadhaa?
> (wah-*weh*-zah koo-ee-teh-ngeh-*neh*-zah
> kwah see-koo kah-th*ah*)

How much does the service cost?
> Bei ya kazi ni nini?
> (*beh*-ee yah *kah*-zee nee *nee*-nee)

Can I buy new parts here?
> Naweza kununua vipande hapa?
> (nah-*weh*-zah koo-noo-*noo*-ah vee-pah-ndeh
> *hah*-pah)

Can you tow the auto?
>Waweza kuvuta motokaa?
>(wah-*weh*-zah koo-*voo*-tah moh-toh-k*ah*)

I have a flat tire.
>Gurudumu langu lina tundu.
>(goo-roo-*doo*-moo lah-ngoo lee-nah *too*-ndoo)

Please change it.
>Tafadhali ligeuze.
>(tah-fah-*thah*-lee lee-geh-*oo*-zeh)

I want the car cleaned.
>Nataka motakaa isafishwe.
>(nah-*tah*-kah moh-toh-k*ah* ee-sah-*fee*-shweh)

Please check the spark plugs.
>Tafadhali angalia sipaki zake.
>(tah-fah-*thah*-lee ah-ngah-*lee*-ah see-pah-kee *zah*-keh)

The motor misses.
>Enjini ina misifuaya.
>(eh-*njee*-nee ee-nah mee-see-foo-*ah*-yah)

My lights are out.
>Taa zangu zimezimika.
>(t*ah* *zah*-ngoo zee-meh-zee-*mee*-kah)

I am in a hurry.
>Nina haraka. (nee-nah hah-*rah*-kah)

Can I leave my car here?
>Naweza kuacha motokaa yangu hapa?
>(nah-*weh*-zah koo-*ah*-chah moh-toh-k*ah* yah-ngoo *hah*-pah)

When shall I return for it?
>Nitarudi kuichukua saa ngapi?
>(nee-tah-*roo*-dee koo-ee-choo-*koo*-ah s*ah* *ngah*-pee)

I need a windshield wiper.
>Nataka kifagio cha mvua.
>(nah-*tah*-kah kee-fah-*gee*-oh chah *mvoo*-ah)

I need a fan belt.
> Nataka kamba ya kipepeo.
> (nah-*tah*-kah *kah*-mbah yah kee-peh-*peh*-oh)

My brake is not working.
> Bireki zangu hazifanyi kazi.
> (bee-reh-kee *zah*-ngoo hah-zee-*fah*-nyee *kah*-zee)

Do you have a gasoline can?
> Una galani ya petroli?
> (oo-nah gah-*lah*-nee yah peh-*troh*-lee)

Do you have a flashlight?
> Una tochi? (oo-nah *toh*-chee)

Is the auto safe for travel?
> Motokaa sawa sawa kwa safari sasa?
> (moh-toh-k*ah* sah-wah *sah*-wah sah-fah-ree *sah*-sah)

DINNER

We would like to find a small quiet place to eat.
    Tungependa kupata mahali padogo penye usa-
lama pa kulia.
    (too-ngeh-*peh*-ndah koo-pah-tah mah-*hah*-lee
pah-doh-goh *peh*-nyeh oo-sah-*lah*-mah pah
koo-*lee*-ah)

We would like a table for four.
    Tungependa meza kwa wanne.
    (too-ngeh-*peh*-ndah *meh*-zah kwah wah-*n*-neh)

I prefer this table.
    Napendelea hii meza.
    (nah-peh-ndeh-*leh*-ah h*ee* meh-zah)

I would like a brandy first.
    Ningependa brandi kwanza.
    (nee-ngeh-*peh*-ndah brah-ndee *kwah*-nzah)

I would like to order now.
    Ningependa kuagiza sasa.
    (nee-ngeh-*peh*-ndah koo-ah-*gee*-zah *sah*-sah)

This is not tasty.
    Hiki hakina utamu.
    (hee-kee hah-*kee*-nah oo-*tah*-moo)

This is delicious.
    Hiki kitamu sana.
    (hee-kee kee-*tah*-moo *sah*-nah)

I would like potatoes.
    Ningependa viazi.
    (nee-ngeh-*peh*-ndah vee-*ah*-zee)

I would like rice.
    Ningependa mchele.
    (nee-ngeh-peh-ndah *mcheh*-leh)

Please bring me another fork.
    Tafadhali niletee uma mwingine.
    (tah-fah-*thah*-lee nee-leh-teh oo-mah
mwee-*ngee*-neh)

another spoon
>kijiko kingine (kee-*jee*-koh kee-*ngee*-neh)

extra napkins
>kitambaacha meza zaidi
>(kee-tah-mbah-*ah*-chah meh-zah zah-*ee*-dee)

May I have a sharper knife?
>Nipate kisu kikali zaidi?
>(nee-pah-teh *kee*-soo kee-kah-lee zah-*ee*-dee)

Please bring my check.
>Tafadhali niletee cheki changu.
>(tah-fah-*thah*-lee nee-leh-teh cheh-kee
>*chah*-ngoo)

Is this correct?
>Hiki ni sawasawa?
>(hee-kee nee sah-wah-*sah*-wah)

Do I pay you or the cashier?
>Nikulipe au kwa daftari?
>(nee-koo-*lee*-peh ah-oo kwah dahf-*tah*-ree)

Is the tip included?
>Bakshishi iko ndani?
>(bahk-*shee*-shee ee-koh *ndah*-nee)

The food was good.
>Chakula kilikuwa kizuri.
>(chah-*koo*-lah kee-lee-*koo*-wah kee-*zoo*-ree)

Please charge this bill to my account.
>Tafadhali tia deni hii kwa orodha yangu.
>(tah-fah-*thah*-lee tee-ah *deh*-nee hee kwah
>oh-*roh*-thah *yah*-ngoo)

This is for you.
>Hiki ni chako. (*hee*-kee nee *chah*-koh)

GETTING ACQUAINTED

Greetings.
> Hujambo. (hoo-*jah*-mboh)

Greetings. (in reply)
> Sijambo (see-*jah*-mboh)

How have you been lately?
> Habari ya siku nyingi?
> (hah-*bah*-ree yah see-koo *nyee*-ngee)

Well, thank you.
> Njema. (*njeh*-mah)

May I come in?
> Hodi? (*hoh*-dee)

Enter.
> Karibu. (kah-*ree*-boo)

Sit down.
> Kaa kitako. (k*ah* kee-*tah*-koh)

Where do you live?
> Unakaa Wapi? (oo-nah-k*ah* *wah*-pee)

Do you speak English?
> Wasema Kiingereza?
> (wah-*seh*-mah kee-ee-ngeh-*reh*-zah)

It does not matter.
> Si neno. (see *neh*-noh)

I go to school.
> Naenda chuoni. (nah-*eh*-ndah choo-*oh*-nee)

Do you have a job?
> Una kazi? (*oo*-nah *kah*-zee)

What is this?
> Hiki ni nini? (*hee*-kee nee *nee*-nee)

Do you have a match?
> Una kiberiti? (*oo*-nah kee-beh-*ree*-tee)

Your city is nice.
> M̄ji wenu ni m̄zuri sana.
> (m̄-jee *weh*-noo nee m̄-*zoo*-ree *sah*-nah)

Have you ever gone to America?
 Umekwenda Amerikani?
 (oo-meh-*kweh*-ndah Ah-meh-ree-*kah*-nee)

Do you like movies?
 Wapenda sinema?
 (wah-*peh*-ndah see-*neh* mah)

Do you like sport?
 Wapenda michezo?
 (wah-*peh*-ndah mee-*cheh*-zoh)

This is my wife.
 Huyu ni m̄ke wangu.
 (*hoo*-yoo nee *m*-keh *wah*-ngoo)

I like your family.
 Napenda watu wa kwenu nyumbani.
 (nah-*peh*-ndah wah-too wah *kweh*-noo
 nyoo-*mbah*-nee)

Do you have children?
 Una watoto? (*oo*-nah wah-*toh*-toh)

You are very pretty.
 U m̄rembo sana. (*ooh* m̄-*reh*-mboh *sah*-nah)

How are things at home?
 Habari gani nyumbani?
 (hah-bah-ree *gah*-nee nyoo-*mbah*-nee)

Who are these people?
 Watu hawa ni nani?
 (*wah*-too hah-wah nee *nah*-nee)

Is he a good man?
 Yeye ni m̄tu mwema?
 (*yeh*-yeh nee *m*-too *mweh*-mah)

Which one?
 M̄tu yupi? (*m*-too *yoo*-pee)

Yes. I have seen him.
 Ndiyo. Nimemwona.
 (*ndee*-yoh. Nee-meh-*mwoh*-nah)

Would you like to go shopping with me?
>Ungependa kwenda madukani pamoja nami?
>(oo-ngeh-*peh*-ndah kweh-ndah
>mah-doo-*kah*-nee pah-*moh*-jah *nah*-mee)

I am troubled.
>Nina mashaka. (*nee*-nah mah-*shah*-kah)

Do you have problems?
>Una mambo? (*oo*-nah *mah*-mboh)

What is going on?
>Jambo gani? (*jah*-mboh *gah*-nee)

My sympathy.
>Pole pole. (poh-leh *poh*-leh)

May I see you again?
>Naweza kukuona tena?
>(nah-*weh*-zah koo-koo-*oh*-nah *teh*-nah)

What is your telephone number?
>Nambari ya simu yako ni nini?
>(nah-*mbah*-ree yah see-moo *yah*-koh nee
>*nee*-nee)

Good luck.
>Bahati njema. (bah-hah-tee *njeh*-mah)

AT THE OFFICE

Are these papers any good?
>Karatasi hizi ni ñzuri?
>(kah-rah-tah-see *hee*-zee nee ñ-*zoo*-ree)

Where should I put them?
>Niiweke wapi? (nee-ee-*weh*-keh *wah*-pee)

These are no good.
>Hizo ni mbaya. (*hee*-zoh nee *mbah*-yah)

Please translate this.
>Tafadhali tafsiri hii.
>(tah-fah-*thah*-lee tahf-*see*-ree h*ee*)

Do you wish it done now?
>Wataka ifanywe sasa?
>(wah-*tah*-kah ee-*fah*-nyweh *sah*-sah)

Please type this letter.
> Tafadhali chapa baruwa hii.
> (tah-fah-*thah*-lee chah-pah bah-*roo*-wah-h*ee*)

Can you finish the work tonight?
> Waweza kuimaliza kazi hii leo usiku.
> (wah-*weh*-zah koo-ee-mah-*lee*-zah kah-zee
> h*ee* leh-oh oo-*see*-koo)

This is well done.
> Hii imefanywa kwa makini.
> (h*ee* ee-meh-*fah*-nywah kwah mah-*kee*-nee)

Are you the boss?
> Wewe ndiwe bwana m̃kubwa?
> (weh-weh *ndee*-weh bwah-nah m̃-*koo*-bwah)

I should like to meet everyone here tomorrow.
> Ningependa kukuta kila m̃tu hapa kesho.
> (nee-ngeh-*peh*-ndah koo-*koo*-tah kee-lah
> *m*-too hah-pah *keh*-shoh)

Coffee break.
> Nafasi ya kahawa.
> nah-*fah*-see yah kah-*hah*-wah)

WHEN YOU ARE SICK

I am ill.
>Ni m̄gonjwa. (*nee m̄-goh*-njwah)

Please get me a doctor.
>Tafadhali nipatie daktari.
>tah-fah-*thah*-lee nee-pah-*tee*-eh dahk-*tah*-ree)

I have a headache.
>Naumia kichwani.
>(nah-oo-*mee*-ah kee-*chwah*-nee)

It hurts here.
>Naumia hapa. (nah-oo-*mee*-ah *hah*-pah)

My stomach hurts.
>Naumia tumboni.
>(nah-oo-*mee*-ah too-*mboh*-nee)

I have a fever.
>Nina homa. (nee-nah *hoh*-mah)

My back hurts.
>M̄gongo waniuma.
>(*mgoh*-ngoh wah-nee-*oo*-mah)

My leg hurts.
>M̄guu waniuma. (mgoo wah-nee-*oo*-mah)

Is it broken?
>Imevunjika? (ee-meh-voo-*njee*-kah)

Is it sprained?
>Imeteguka? (ee-meh-teh-*goo*-kah)

I burned myself.
>Nimejiunguza. (nee-meh-jee-oo-*ngoo*-zah)

I hurt all over.
>Naumia kila mahali.
>(nah-oo-*mee*-ah kee-lah mah-*hah*-lee)

I feel chilled.
>Naona baridi. (nah-*oh*-nah bah-*ree*-dee)

I have diarrhea
Ninahara. (nee-nah-*hah*-rah)

Will I have to be hospitalized?
Natakwenda hospitalini?
(nah-tah-*kweh*-ndah hohs-pee-tah-*lee*-nee)

I have something in my eye.
Nina kidude jichoni.
(nee-nah kee-*doo*-deh jee-*choh*-nee)

Can you give me some medicine?
Waweza kunipa dawa?
(wah-*weh*-zah koo-nee-pah *dah*-wah)

Will I be able to travel?
Nitaweza kusafiri?
(nee-tah-*weh*-zah koo-sah-*fee*-ree)

The pain started yesterday.
Uchungu ulianza jana.
(oo-*choo*-ngoo oo-lee-*ah*-nzah *jah*-nah)

Lie on this table.
Lala juu ya meza. (lah-lah joo yah *meh*-zah)

Open your mouth.
Fungua m̃domo wako.
(foo-*ngoo*-ah *mdoh*-moh *wah*-koh)

Breathe hard
Pumua kwa nguvu.
(poo-*moo*-ah kwah *ngoo*-voo)

You must stay in bed.
Lazima ulale. (lah-*zee*-mah oo-*lah*-leh)

Do you feel better now?
Waona nafuu sasa?
(wah-*oh*-nah nah-foo *sah*-sah)

THE DENTIST

I have a toothache.
Naumia jino. (nah-oo-*mee*-ah *jee*-noh)

I am in great pain.
> Naona uchungu sana.
> (nah-*oh*-nah oo-*choo*-ngoo *sah*-nah)

Do you have to extract it?
> Wataka kuitoa? (wah-*tah*-kah koo-ee-*toh*-ah)

Can you give me some aspirin?
> Waweza kunipa aspirini?
> wah-*weh*-zah koo-*nee*-pah ahs-pee-*ree*-nee)

THE OPTICIAN

I want a pair of sunglasses.
> Nataka miwani ya jua.
> (nah-*tah*-kah mee-*wah*-nee yah *joo*-ah)

I need them fitted.
> Nataka ikamilishwe.
> (nah-*tah*-kah ee-kah-mee-*lee*-shweh)

I need them immediately.
> Naitaka haraka. (nah-ee-*tah*-kah hah-*rah*-kah)

What is your fee?
> Malipo yako ni nini?
> (mah-lee-poh *yak*-koh nee *nee*-nee)

PERSONAL NEEDS

AT THE BARBER SHOP

Can you give me a haircut?
    Waweza   kuninyoa?
    (wah-*weh*-zah koo-nee-*nyoh*-ah)

I like it short.
    Naitaka fupi. (nah-ee-*tah*-kah *foo*-pee)

I like it long.
    Naitaka ndefu. (nah-ee-*tah*-kah *ndeh*-foo)

Cut a little more off the sides.
    Kata zaidi kidogo upande.
    (kah-tah zah-*ee*-dee kee-*doh*-goh oo-*pah*-ndeh)

the back   *the top*
    nyuma (*nyoo*-mah)   juu (j*oo*)

I want a shave.
    Nataka ninyolewe ndevu.
    (nah-*tah*-kah nee-nyoh-*leh*-weh *ndeh*-voo)

I want a shampoo.
    Nataka shampu. (nah-*tah*-kah *shah*-mpoo)

AT THE BEAUTY SHOP

I want my hair shampooed.
    Nataka kuosha manyele.
    (nah-*tah*-kah koo-oh-shah mah-*nyeh*-leh)

and set
    na kupanga (nah koo-*pah*-ngah)

I want a facial.
    Nataka cha mechoni.
    (nah-*tah*-kah chah meh-*choh*-nee)

45

I want a permanent.
      Nataka ya kudumu.
      (nah-*tah*-kah yah koo-*doo*-moo)
The water is too hot.
      Maji haya moto sana.
      (mah-jee *hah*-yah moh-toh *sah*-nah)
too cold
      baridi sana (bah-*ree*-dee *sah*-nah)

How long will I have to wait?
      Nitangoja muda gani?
      (nee-tah-*ngoh*-jah moo-dah-*gah*-nee)

When can you give me an appointment?
      Tuagane nije lini?
      (too-ah-*gah*-neh nee-jeh *lee*-nee)

How much do I owe you?
      Nina deni gani? (*nee*-nah deh-nee *gah*-nee)

PUBLIC SERVICE

USING THE TELEPHONE

Hello.
> Helo. (*heh*-loh)

Who is speaking?
> Nani asema? (*nah*-nee ah-*seh*-mah)

I wish to speak to............
> Nataka kusema na............
> (nah-*tah*-kah koo-*seh*-mah nah............)

Please tell him I called.
> Tafadhali umwambie niliita.
> (tah-fah-*thah*-lee oo-mwah-*mbee*-eh
> nee-lee-*ee*-tah)

My number is............
> Namba yangu ni............
> (nah-mbah *yah*-ngoo nee............)

I want extension............
> Nataka kitengo la............
> (nah-*tah*-kah kee-*teh*-ngoh lah............)

There is no answer.
> Hakuna majibu. (hah-*koo*-nah mah-*jee*-boo)

You have the wrong number.
> Una nambari isiyo sawa.
> (oo-nah nah-*mbah*-ree ee-*see*-yoh *sah*-wah)

The line is busy.
> Laini si huru. (lah-*ee*-nee see *hoo*-roo)

I shall call back.
> Nitaita baadaye.
> (nee-tah-*ee*-tah bah-ah-*dah*-yeh)

SENDING A CABLE

Where can I send a cablegram?
> Naweza kutuma simu wapi?
> (nah-*weh*-zah koo-*too*-mah see-moo *wah*-pee)

47

What is the cost per word?
> Ni bei gani kila neno?
> (nee beh-ee *gah*-nee kee-lah *neh*-noh)

I want to pay for it now.
> Nataka kuilipia sasa.
> (nah-*tah*-kah koo-ee-lee-*pee*-ah *sah*-sah)

How much is a night cable?
> Simu ya usiku ni bei gani?
> (*see*-moo yah oo-*see*-koo nee beh-ee *gah*-nee)

AT THE POST OFFICE

Where is the Post Office?
> Posta iko wapi? (*poh*-stah ee-koh *wah*-pee)

What does it cost to send this letter air-mail?
> Bei ya baruwa kwa ndege ni nini?
> (*beh*-ee yah bah-*roo*-wah kwah *ndeh*-geh
> nee *nee*-nee)

I want some postcards.
> Nataka kadi kadhaa.
> (nah-*tah*-kah *kah*-dee kah-th*ah*)

I want to register this letter.
> Nataka kutia baruwa hii muhuri.
> (nah-*tah*-kah koo-tee-ah bah-*roo*-wah
> hee moo-*hoo*-ree)

Please give me .... worth of stamps.
> Tafadhali nipe sitampu ya.............
> (tah-fah-*thah*-lee nee-peh see-*tah*-mpoo
> yah ....)

I want an air-mail envelope.
> Nataka bahasha ya ndege.
> (nah-*tah*-kah bah-*hah*-shah yah *ndeh*-geh)

Regular postage.
> Posta ya kawaida.
> (*poh*-stah yah kah-wah-*ee*-dah)

MONEY

I want to change some American money.
>Nataka kugeuza pesa za Kiamerika.
>(nah-*tah*-kah koo-geh-uzah *peh*-sah zah
>kee-ah-meh-*ree*-kah)

Is there a bank close by?
>Kuna bengi karibuni?
>(koo-nah *beh*-ngee kah-ree-*boo*-nee)

What is the rate to the dollar?
>Dola moja ni pesa ngapi?
>(doh-lah *moh*-jah nee *peh*-sah *ngah*-pee)

Do you accept Traveler's checks?
>Wachukua cheki za wasafiri?
>(wah-choo-*koo*-ah *cheh*-kee zah
>wah-sah-*fee*-ree)

Here is my identification.
>Mafumbuo yangu ni haya.
>(mah-foo-*mboo*-oh *yah*-ngoo nee *hah*-yah)

Sign here.
>Tia kidole hapa. (tee-ah kee-*doh*-leh *hah*-pah)

Please give me a receipt.
>Tafadhali nipe risiti.
>(tah-fah-*thah*-lee nee-peh ree-*see*-tee)

I want to change ten dollars.
>Nataka kugenza dola kumi.
>(nah-*tah*-kah koo-*geh*-nzah doh-lah *koo*-mee)

I have a bank note.
>Nina noti ya bengi.
>(nee-nah *noh*-tee yah *beh*-ngee)

I want to open an account.
>Nataka kanza daftari.
>(nah-*tah*-kah kwah-nzah dahf-*tah*-ree)

Do you have any small change?
>Una pesa ndogo? (oo-nah *peh*-sah *ndoh*-goh)

Can I get a money order here?
>Naweza kupata manioda hapa?
>(nah-weh-zah koo-*pah*-tah mah-nee-*oh*-dah
>*hah*-pah)

49

WHEN YOU ARE SHOPPING

I want to buy a watch.
>   Nataka kununua saa ya mkono.
>   (nah-*tah*-kah koo-noo-*noo*-ah s*a*h yah
>   m*koh*-noh)

It is for a man.
>   Ni kwa bwana. (nee kwah *bwah*-nah)

It is for a woman.
>   Ni kwa bibi. (nee kwah *bee*-bee)

I am only looking now.
>   Ninachungulia sasa hivi.
>   (nee-nah-choo-ngoo-*lee*-ah sah-sah *hee*-vee)

This is all that I want.
>   Hivi tu ndivyo nataka.
>   (*hee*-vee too *ndee*-vyoh nah-*tah*-kah)

I want to buy ....
>   Nataka kununua ....
>   (nah-*tah*-kah koo-noo-*noo*-ah)

shoes
>   viatu (vee-*ah*-too)

boots
>   viatu vya matope
>   (vee-*ah*-too vyah mah-*toh*-peh)

a present
>   zawadi (zah-wah-dee)

a bracelet
>   kiringa cha mkono
>   (kee-*ree*-ngah chah m*koh*-noh)

a necklace
>   almasi ya shingoni
>   (ahl-*mah*-see yah shee-*ngoh*-nee)

earrings
>   almasi ya masikio
>   (ahl-*mah*-see yah mah-see-*kee*-oh)

50

perfume
>marashi (mah-*rah*-shee)

cigarettes
>sigara (see-*gah*-rah)

a hat
>kofia (koh-*fee*-ah)

a suit
>suti (*soo*-tee)

a dress
>nguo (*ngoo*-oh)

I would like a shirt.
>Ningependa shati.
>(nee-ngeh-*peh*-ndah *shah*-tee)

Please wrap it.
>Tafadhali funga.
>(tah-fah-*thah*-lee *foo*-ngah)

I would like............ .
>Ningependa........ . (nee-ngeh-peh-ndah........)

a blouse
>bilausi (bee-lah-*oo*-see)

a jacket
>koti (*koh*-tee)

underwear
>nguo cha ndani (*ngoo*-oh chah *ndah*-nee)

a belt
>kamba (*kah*-mbah)

a raincoat
>kabuti (kah-*boo*-tee)

How much is this?
>Hii ni bei gani? (hee nee beh-ee *gah*-nee)

I like this one.
>Napenda hii. (nah-*peh*-ndah hee)

I do not like this color.
>Sitaki rangi hii. (see-*tah*-kee rah-ngee hee)

I want it in white.
>Nataka nyeupe. (nah-*tah*-kah nyeh-*oo*-peh)

yellow
>manjano (mah-*njah*-noh)

brown
>kunde (*koo*-ndeh)

blue
>buluu (boo-loo)

red
>nyekundu (nyeh-*koo*-ndoo)

black
>nyeusi (nyeh-*oo*-see)

gray
>giree (gee-reh)

I do not like this style.
>Sipendi staili hii.
>(see-*peh*-ndee stah-*ee*-lee hee)

May I try this on?
>Naweza kujaribu hii.
>(nah-*weh*-zah koo-jah-*ree*-boo hee)

It doesn't fit well.
>Hainitoshi. (hah-ee-nee-*toh*-shee)

It is too large.
>Ni kubwa zaidi. (nee *koo*-bwah zah-*ee*-dee)

It is too small.
>Ni ndogo zaidi. (nee *ndoh*-goh zah-*ee*-dee)

It is too tight.
>Inaringa sana. (ee-nah-*ree*-ngah *sah*-nah)

Is this a bargain?
>Hii ni ya kupiga bei? (Hee nee yah
>koo-*pee*-gah *beh*-ee)

This is too expensive.
>Hii ni bei ghali sana.
>(hee nee beh-ee *ghah*-lee *sah*-nah)

I would like something cheaper.
>   Napenda kitu rahisi.
>   (nah-*peh*-ndah kee-too rah-*hee*-see)

I want clothing for a boy.
>   Nataka nguo kwa kijana.
>   (nah-*tah*-kah *ngoo*-oh kwah kee-*jah*-nah)

a girl
>   msichana (msee-*chah*-nah)

a baby
>   m̄toto (*mtoh*-toh)

I don't know her size.
>   Sijui mipimo yake.
>   (see-*joo*-ee mee-*pee*-moh *yah*-keh)

The boy is five years old.
>   Kijana ana miaka mitano.
>   (kee-*jah*-nah ah-nah mee-*ah*-kah mee-*tah*-noh)

Do you have books?
>   Una vitabu? (*oo*-nah vee-*tah*-boo)

Do you have toys?
>   Una vidude vya watoto?
>   (oo-nah vee-*doo*-deh vyah wah-*toh*-toh)

I shall take it with me.
>   Nitachukua pamoja nami.
>   (nee-tah-choo-*koo*-ah pah-moh-jah *nah*-mee)

CAMERAS AND FILM

I want to buy a camera.
>   Nataka kununua picha.
>   (nah-*tah*-kah koo-noo noo-ah *pee*-chah)

I want to buy some film.
>   Nataka kununua filmi nyingine.
>   (nah-*tah*-kah koo-noo-*noo*-ah feel-mee
>   nyee-*ngee*-neh)

Do you have American size film?
>   Una filmi kiamerika?
>   (oo-nah *feel*-mee kee-ah-meh-*ree*-kah)

How much is it?
>Bei yake ni nini? (*beh*-ee yah-keh nee *nee*-nee)

I want a roll of color film.
>Nataka filmi ya rangi.
>(nah-tah-kah *feel*-mee yah *rah*-ngee)

I want to buy a movie camera.
>Nataka kununua picha ya sinema.
>(nah-*tah*-kah koo-noo-*noo*-ah pee-chah yah
>see-*neh*-mah

I would like these pictures developed.
>Ningependa picha hizi zitengenezwe.
>(nee-ngeh-*peh*-ndah pee-chah *hee*-zee
>zee-teh-ngeh-*neh*-zweh)

I would like an enlargement.
>Nataka zifanywe kubwa.
>(nah-*tah*-kah zee-fah-nyweh *koo*-bwah)

When will they be ready?
>Zitakuwa tayari lini?
>(zee-tah-*koo*-wah tah-yah-ree *lee*-nee)

Can you repair my camera?
>Waweza kutengeneza picha yangu?
>(wah-*weh*-zah koo-teh-ngeh-*neh*-zah pee-chah
>*yah*-ngoo)

SHOE REPAIR

I want these shoes repaired.
>Nataka viatu hivi vitengenezwe.
>(nah-*tah*-kah vee-ah-too *hee*-vee
>vee-teh-ngeh-*neh*-zweh)

I want a rubber heel.
>Nataka kisigino cha mpira.
>(nah-*tah*-kah kee-see-*gee*-noh chah *mpee*-rah)

a leather heel
>Kisigino cha ngozi
>(kee-see-*gee*-noh chah *ngoh*-zee)

I want them half-soled.
>Nataka nusu ya kisigino kiongezwe.
>(nah-tah-kah *noo*-soo yah kee-see-*gee*-noh
>kee-oh-*ngeh*-zweh)

When will they be ready?
>Vitakuwa tayari lini?
>(vee-tah-*koo*-wah tah-*yah*-ree *lee*-nee)

NEWSPAPERS AND MAGAZINES

I would like a morning paper.
>Ningependa magazeti ya asubuhi.
>(nee-ngeh-*peh*-ndah mah-gah-*zeh*-tee yah
>ah-soo-*boo*-hee)

Do you have American newspapers?
>Una magazeti ya Kiamerika?
>(*oo*-nah mah-gah-*zeh*-tee yah
>kee-ah-meh-*ree*-kah)

Which is the best newspaper?
>Gazeti zuri zaidi ni lipi?
>(gah-zeh-tee *zoo*-ree zah-*ee*-dee nee *lee*-pee)

EMERGENCIES

Police!
> Polisi! (poh-*lee*-see)

Fire!
> Moto! (*moh*-toh)

Look!
> Angalia! (ah-ngah-*lee*-ah)

Stop!
> Simama! (see-*mah*-mah)

Get Out!
> Simile! (see-*mee*-leh)

Help me!
> Nisaidie! (nee-sah-ee-*dee*-eh)

A man robbed me!
> M̄tu aliniibia! (*m*-too ah-lee-nee-ee-*bee*-ah)

There has been an accident!
> Kumekuwa na hatari!
> (koo-meh-*koo*-wah nah hah-*tah*-ree)

Call a doctor!
> Mwite daktari! (*mwee*-teh dahk-*tah*-ree)

Are you all right?
> Wewe sawa sawa? (*weh*-weh sah-wah *sah*-wah)

I have lost my passport.
> Nimepoteza pasipoti yangu.
> (nee-meh-poh-*teh*-zah pah-see-*poh*-tee
> *yah*-ngoo)

What has happened?
> Kumetokea nini?
> (koo-meh-toh-*keh*-ah *nee*-nee)

Stop that person!
> Mkamate m̄tu huyo!
> (mkah-*mah*-teh *m*-too *hoo*-yoh)

I cannot find my child.
> Siwezi kumpata m̄toto wangu.
> (see-*weh*-zee koo-*mpah*-tah m̄toh-toh
> *wah*-ngoo)

SIGHTSEEING

Is there a guide service?
Kuna waongozi? (*koo*-nah wah-oh-*ngoh*-zee)

Where are the museums?
Musiami iko wapi?
(moo-see-*ah*-mee ee-koh *wah*-pee)

Where are the theaters?
Sinema ziko wapi?
(see-*neh*-mah zee-koh *wah*-pee)

Is admission free?
Hakuna nauli ya kuingia?
(hah-koo-nah nah-*oo*-lee yah koo-ee-*ngee*-ah)

Are there any churches near here?
Kuna kanisa zozote karibuni?
(*koo*-nah kah-nee-sah zoh-*zoh*-teh
kah-ree-*boo*-nee)

May I take photographs?
Naweza kupiga mapicha?
(nah-*weh*-zah koo-pee-gah mah-*pee*-chah)

This sight is beautiful.
Hapa ni pazuri. (hah-pah nee pah-*zoo*-ree)

How old is this place?
Mahali hapa ni pa miaka mingapi?
mah-hah-lee *hah*-pah nee pah mee-*ah*-kah
mee-*ngah*-pee)

May I go in?
Niingie? (nee-ee-*ngee*-eh)

NIGHT LIFE

Is there a good night club here?
Kuna nyumba ya kilabu zuri hapa?
(koo-nah *nyoo*-mbah yah kee-*lah*-boo *zoo*-ree
hah-pah)

Is there a show tonight?
Kuna maonyesho leo?
(*koo*-nah mah-oh-*nyeh*-shoh *leh*-oh)

What time does the show begin?
Maonyesho yaanza saa ngapi?
(mah-oh-*nyeh*-shoh yah-*ah*-nzah sah *ngah*-pee)

When is it finished?
Huisha saa ngapi? (hoo-*ee*-shah sah *ngah*-pee)

Do they serve dinner at the club?
Kuna vyakula kilabuni?
(*koo*-nah vyah-*koo*-lah kee-lah-*boo*-nee)

Is there a door charge?
Kuna nauli ya mlangoni?
(*koo*-nah nah-*oo*-lee yah mlah-*ngoh*-nee)

May I have this dance?
Ungependa kucheza huu sasa?
(oo-ngeh-*peh*-ndah koo-*cheh*-zah hoo *sah*-sah)

The entertainment is nice.
Mchezo huu ni mzuri sana.
(mcheh-zoh hoo nee m̄zoo-ree *sah*-nah)

SPORTS

Where is the lake?
> Ziwa iko wapi? (*zee*-wah ee-koh *wah*-pee)

May I swim in the lake?
> Naweza kuogelea ziwani?
> (nah-*weh*-zah koo-oh-geh-*leh*-ah zee-*wah*-nee)

The water is wonderful.
> Maji haya ni ya ajabu.
> (mah-jee *hah*-yah nee yah ah-*jah*-boo)

The water is rough.
> Maji yame. (mah-jee yah-meh)

Where can I get towels?
> Naweza kupata taulo wapi?
> (nah-weh-zah koo-*pah*-tah tah-*oo*-loh *wah*-pee)

I want to lie in the sun.
> Nataka kulala juani.
> (nah-*tah*-kah koo-lah-lah joo-*ah*-nee)

Is there a tennis court near here?
> Kuna kiwanja cha tenisi karibuni?
> (*koo*-nah kee-*wah*-njah chah teh-*nee*-see
> kah-ree-*boo*-nee)

Can I rent equipment?
> Naweza kukomboa vyombo?
> (nah-*weh*-zah koo-*koh-mboh*-ah *vyoh*-mboh)

TIME AND DATES

What time is it?
> Ni saa ngapi? (nee s*ah* *ngah*-pee)

Morning
> Asubuhi (ah-soo-*boo*-hee)

Evening
> Jioni (jee-*oh*-nee)

Noon
> Adhuhuri (ah-thoo-*hoo*-ree)

Is your watch correct?
> Saa yako ni sawa sawa?
> (s*ah* *yah*-koh nee sah-wah *sah*-wah)

My watch is slow.
> Saa yangu imechelewa.
> (s*ah* *yah*-ngoo ee-meh-cheh-*leh*-wah)

It is twelve noon.
> Ni saa sita adhuhuri.
> (nee s*ah* see-tah ah-thoo-*hoo*-ree)

It is six o'clock (pm).
> Ni saa kumi na mbili.
> (nee s*ah* koo-mee nah *mbee*-lee)

It is midnight.
> Ni usiku wa manane.
> (nee oo-*see*-koo wah mah-*nah*-neh)

I am late.
> Nimechelewa. (nee-meh-cheh-*leh*-wah)

I am early.
> Ni mapema. (nee mah-*peh*-mah)

DATES

Today
> Leo (*leh*-oh)

Yesterday
> Jana (*jah*-nah)

60

Tomorrow
> Kesho (*keh*-shoh)

Day after tomorrow
> Kesho kutwa (*keh*-shoh *koo*-twah)

Tomorrow morning
> Kesho asubuhi (*keh*-shoh ah-soo-*boo*-hee)

Tonight
> Leo usiku (*leh*-oh oo-*see*-koo)

Last night
> Jana usiku (*jah*-nah oo-*see*-koo)

Last week
> Juma jana (*joo*-mah *jah*-nah)

Next week
> Juma lijalo (*joo*-mah lee-*jah*-loh)

Everyday
> Kila siku (kee-lah *see*-koo)

In a few days
> Kwa siku chache (kwah *see*-koo *chah*-cheh)

Last month
> Mwezi jana (*mweh*-zee *jah*-nah)

Every other day
> Kila siku la pili (kee-lah *see*-koo lah *pee*-lee)

Saturday
> Jumamosi (joo-mah-*moh*-see)

Sunday
> Jumapili (joo-mah-*pee*-lee)

Monday
> Jumatatu (joo-mah-*tah*-too)

Tuesday
> Jumanne (joo-mah-*n*-neh)

Wednesday
> Jumatano (joo-mah-*tah*-noh)

Thursday
> Alhamisi (ahl-hah-*mee*-see)

Friday
> Ijumaa (ee-joo-*mah*)

WEATHER

The weather is good.
> Hali ya hewa ni njema.
> (*hah*-lee yah *heh*-wah nee *njeh*-mah)

The weather is bad.
> Hali ya hewa ni mbaya.
> (*hah*-lee yah *heh*-wah nee *mbah*-yah)

It looks like rain.
> Huonekana itanyesha.
> (hoo-oh-neh-*kah*-nah ee-tah-*nyeh*-shah)

Is it always this warm here?
> Ni joto hapa hivi kila siku?
> (nee *joh*-toh hah-pah *hee*-vee kee-lah *see*-koo)

Does it get cooler?
> Huwa baridi? (*hoo*-wah bah-*ree*-dee)

It is very windy.
> Upepo huvuma sana.
> (oo-*peh*-poh hoo-*voo*-mah *sah*-nah)

It is raining hard.
> Mvua hunyesha sana.
> (*mvoo*-ah hoo-*nyeh*-shah *sah*-nah)

The sky is clear.
> Mbingu ni tupu. (*mbee*-ngoo nee *too*-poo)

The sun is shining today
> Jua uko leo. (*joo*-ah oo-koh *leh*-oh)

The stars are out tonight.
> Nyota zimejitoa leo.
> (*nyoh*-tah zee-meh-jee-*toh*-ah *leh*-oh)

I like this weather.
> Napenda hali hii. (nah-*peh*-ndah hah-lee hee)

VOCABULARY

able (*to be*)	kuweza (koo-*weh*-zah)
aboard	pakia (pah-*kee*-ah)
about (*talking*)	habari ya (hah-*bah*-ree yah)
above	juu (joo)
abroad	ugenini (oo-geh-*nee*-nee)
absent	kosea (koh-*seh*-ah)
absolute	kamili (kah-*mee*-lee)
absolutely	kwa ukamilifu
	(kwah oo-kah-mee-*lee*-foo)
academy	shule (*shoo*-leh)
accelerator	mwendeo (mweh-*ndeh*-oh)
accent	msemo wa kigeni
	(*mseh*-moh wah kee-*geh*-nee)
accept (*to*)	kukubalia (koo-koo-bah-*lee*-ah)
accident	ajali (ah-*jah*-lee)
account	mpango wa hesabu
	(*mpah*-ngoh wah heh-*sah*-boo)
ache	umio (oo-*mee*-oh)
acquaintance	ujuzi (oo-*joo*-zee)
across	ng'ambo (ng'*ah*-mboh)
act	tendo (*teh*-ndoh)
active	wa kutenda (wah koo-*teh*-ndah)
actor	mwigaji (mwee-*gah*-jee)
actress	mwigaji wa kike
	(mwee-*gah*-jee wah *kee*-keh)
actual	halisi (hah-*lee*-see)
anxious	kuwa na mashaka
	(*koo*-wah nah mah-*shah*-kah)
anybody	wo wote (woh *woh*-teh)
anything	kitu cho chote (*kee*-too choh *choh*-teh)
anywhere	po pote (poh *poh*-teh)
apology	juto (*joo*-toh)
appear	onekana (oh-neh-*kah*-nah)
appetite	uchu wa chakula
	(*oo*-choo wah chah-*koo*-lah)

63

approve (to)	kukubalia (koo-koo-bah-*lee*-ah)
approximately	kama (*kah*-mah)
arcade	kijia (kee-*jee*-ah)
arch	tao (*tah*-oh)
archbishop	askofu mkuu (ah-*skoh*-foo mkoo)
architect	mtaalam wa ujenzi
	(mtah-*ah*-lam wa oo-*jeh*-nzee)
area	eneo (eh-*neh*-oh)
argue (to)	kujadili (koo-jah-*dee*-lee)
arm	mkono (*mkoh*-noh)
around	kwa mviringo
	(kwah mvee-*ree*-ngoh)
arrange (to)	kutayarisha (koo-tah-yah-*ree*-shah)
arrest	kamata (kah-*mah*-tah)
arrival	kufika kwa (koo-*fee*-kah kwah)
arrive (to)	kufika (koo-*fee*-kah)
art	mchoro (*mchoh*-roh),
	ustadu, (oo-*stah*-doo)
article	kitu (*kee*-too)
artificial	si asili (see ah-*see*-lee)
artist	mstadi (*mstah*-dee)
ashamed	aibishwa (ah-ee-*bee*-shwah)
ask (to)	kuuliza (koo-oo-*lee*-zah)
asleep	kulala (koo-*lah*-lah)
aspirin	aspirini (ah-spee-*ree*-nee)
assistant	msaidizi (msah-ee-*dee*-zee)
association	ushirika (oo-shee-*ree*-kah)
assure	yakinisha (yah-kee-*nee*-shah)
at	kwa (kwah)
athletics	michezo (mee-*cheh*-zoh)
Atlantic	Atlantiki (aht-lah-*ntee*-kee)
atmosphere	hewa (*heh*-wah)
attach	unga (*oo*-ngah)
attempt	jaribu (jah-*ree*-boo)
attend	hudhuria (hoo-thoo-*ree*-ah)
attention	usikizi (oo-see-*kee*-zee)
aunt	shangazi (shah-*ngah*-zee)
author	mtungaji (mtoo-*ngah*-jee)

authority	nguvu (*ngoo*-voo)
automobile	motakari (moh-tah-*kah*-ree)
available	kuwako (koo-*wah*-koh)
average	wastani (wah-*stah*-nee)
avoid	epuka (eh-*poo*-kah)
await	ngojea (ngoh-*jeh*-ah)
awake	amka (ah-*mkah*)
axle	kidude cha kati ya gurudumu (kee-*doo*-deh chah *kah*-tee yah goo-roo-*doo*-moo)
baby	mtoto (*mtoh*-toh)
bachelor	mvulana (mvoo-*lah*-nah)
back	nyuma (*nyoo*-mah)
bacon	nyama ya nguruwe (*nyah*-mah yah ngoo-*roo*-weh)
bad	mbaya (*mbah*-yah)
baggage	mizigo (mee-*zee*-goh)
balcony	roshani (roh-*shah*-nee)
ball	mpira (*mpee*-rah)
banana	ndizi (*ndee*-zee)
bandit	haramia (hah-rah-*mee*-ah)
bank	bengi (*beh*-ngee)
banquet	karamu (kah-*rah*-moo)
bar	kilabu (kee-*lah*-boo)
bargain	kupiga bei (koo-*pee*-gah *beh*-ee)
basket	kikapu (kee-*kah*-poo)
bath	birika ya kuogea (bee-*ree*-kah yah koo-oh-*geh*-ah)
bathroom	chumba cha kuogea (*choo*-mbah chah koo-oh-*geh*-ah)
battery	biteri (bee-*teh*-ree)
battle	vita (*vee*-tah)
be	kuwa (*koo*-wah)
beach	pwani (*pwah*-nee)
beans	kunde (*koo*-ndeh)
beard	ndevu (*ndeh*-voo)

beautiful	mrembo (*mreh*-mboh)
beauty parlor	chumba cha urembo
	(*choo*-mbah chah oo-*reh*-mboh)
because	kwa sababu (kwah sah-*bah*-boo)
bed	kitanda (kee-*tah*-ndah)
bedroom	chumba cha kulala
	(*choo*-mbah chah koo-*lah*-lah)
beef	nyama (*nyah*-mah)
beer	pombe, tembo
	(*poh*-mbeh), (*teh*-mboh)
before	kabla ya (*kah*-blah yah)
beggar	mwombaji (mwoh-*mbah*-jee)
begin	anza (*ah*-nzah)
behind	nyuma ya (*nyoo*-mah yah)
believe	amini (ah-*mee*-nee)
bell	kengele (keh-*ngeh*-leh)
belongs	wa (w*ah*)
belt	kamba (*kah*-mbah)
beside	na tena, kando
	(nah *teh*-nah), (*kah*-ndoh)
best	nzuri zaidi (*nzoo*-ree zah-*ee*-dee)
between	katikati ya (*kah*-tee-*kah*-tee yah)
bicycle	baisikeli (bah-ee-see-*keh*-lee)
big	kubwa (*koo*-bwah)
bill	malipo (mah-*lee*-poh)
bird	ndege (*ndeh*-geh)
birth	zao (*zah*-oh)
birthday	siku ya kuzaliwa
	(*see*-koo yah koo-zah-*lee*-wah)
black	-eusi (-eh-*oo*-see)
blanket	barangeti (bah-rah-*ngeh*-tee)
block	dude (*doo*-deh)
blood	damu (*dah*-moo)
blue	buluu (boo-l*oo*)
boarding house	nyumba ya kulalia
	(*nyoo*-mbah yah koo-lah-*lee*-ah)
boat	shua (*shoo*-ah)
body	mwili (*mwee*-lee)

boil	chemka (*cheh*-mkah)
bomb	bomu (*boh*-moo)
bone	mfupa (*mfoo*-pah)
book	kitabu (kee-*tah*-boo)
bookstore	duka la vitabu
	(*doo*-kah lah vee-*tah*-boo)
border	mpaka (*mpah*-kah)
born	zaliwa (zah-*lee*-wah)
both	wote wawili (*woh*-teh wah-*wee*-lee)
bottle	chupa (*choo*-pah)
bottle opener	kifunguo cha chupa
	(kee-foo-*ngoo*-oh chah *choo*-pah)
bottom	chini (*chee*-nee)
box	sanduku (sah-*ndoo*-koo)
boy	kijana (kee-*jah*-nah)
bracelet	bangili (bah-*ngee*-lee)
brain	ubongo (oo-*boh*-ngoh)
brake	bireki (bee-*reh*-kee)
brave	shujaa (shoo-*jah*)
bread	mkate (*mkah*-teh)
break	vunja (*voo*-njah)
breakfast	chamshakinywa
	(chah-mshah-*kee*-nywah)
breast	titi (*tee*-tee)
breath	pumzi (*poo*-mzee)
bridge	daraja (dah-*rah*-jah)
bright	cha kung'aa (*chah* koo-ng'*ah*)
bring (to)	kileta (kee-*leh*-tah)
broken	vunjika (voo-*njee*-kah)
brother	ndugu (*ndoo*-goo)
brown	majani makavu
	(mah-*jah*-nee mah-*kah*-voo)
brush	sugua (soo-*goo*-ah)
burn	unguza (oo-*ngoo*-zah)
business	biashara (bee-ah-*shah*-rah)
busy	enye kazi (*eh*-nyeh *kah*-zee)
but	lakini (lah-*kee*-nee)
butter	siagi (see-*ah*-gee)

button	funguo (foo-*ngoo*-oh)
buy	nunua (noo-*noo*-ah)
by	kando ya (*kah*-ndoh yah)
cabaret	mchezo wa mkahawani
	(*mcheh*-zoh wah mkah-hah-*wah*-nee)
cable	amari (ah-*mah*-ree)
café	mkahawa (mkah-*hah*-wah)
cake	keki (*keh*-kee)
call	ita (*ee*-tah)
camera	picha (*pee*-chah)
can	mkebe (*mkeh*-beh)
can opener	kifunguo cha mkebe
	(kee-foo-*ngoo*-oh chah *mkeh*-beh)
canal	mfereji (mfeh-*reh*-jee)
cancel	tangua, futia mbali
	(tah-ngoo-ah), foo-tee-ah mbah-lee)
candy	kashata (kah-*shah*-tah)
capital	mji mkuu (m̄jee mkoo)
car	motakari (moh-tah-*kah*-ree)
card	cheti (*cheh*-tee)
care	hadhari (hah-*thah*-ree)
carry	chukua, beba (choo-*koo*-ah),
	(*beh*-bah)
cash	peza (*peh*-zah)
cashier	mtoa peza (*mtoh*-ah *peh*-zah)
cat	paka (*pah*-kah)
catch	shika (shee-kah)
cathedral	kanisa (kah-*nee*-sah)
Catholic	katholiki (Kah-thoh-*lee*-kee)
cattle	ng'ombe (ng'*oh*-mbeh)
cave	pango (*pah*-ngoh)
ceiling	dari (*dah*-ree)
cemetery	kaburini (kah-boo-*ree*-nee)
center	katikati (*kah*-tee-*kah*-tee)
century	karne (*kahr*-neh)
certain	yakini (vah-*kee*-nee)
certificate	hati (*hah*-tee)

chair	kiti (kee-tee)
champagne	divai ya kifaransa
	(dee-*vah*-ee yah kee-fah-*rah*-nsah)
change	geuzo (geh-*oo*-zoh)
chapel	kanisa (kah-*nee*-sah)
charge	ulinzi (oo-*lee*-nzee)
charming	mwenye talasimu
	(*mweh*-nyeh tah-lah-*see*-moo)
chauffeur	dereva (deh-*reh*-vah)
cheap	rahisi (rah-*hee*-see)
cheese	chisi (*chee*-see)
chest	kufua (*koo*-foo-ah)
chicken	kuku (*koo*-koo)
child	mtoto (*mtoh*-toh)
chocolate	kakao (kah-*kah*-oh)
chop	kata (*kah*-tah)
Christian	Mkristo (*mkree*-stoh)
Christmas	Sikukuu (see-koo-koo)
church	kanisa (kah-*nee*-sah)
cigarette	sigara (see-*gah*-rah)
cigar	sigaa (see-*gah*)
circle	mviringo (mvee-*ree*-ngoh)
citizen	raia (rah-*ee*-ah)
city	mji (*m*jee)
class	darasa (dah-*rah*-sah)
clean	safi (*sah*-fee)
climb	panda (*pah*-ndah)
clock	saa (*sah*)
close	karibu (kah-*ree*-boo)
closet	kijumba cha faragha
	(kee-*joo*-mbah chah fah-*rah*-ghah)
cloth	nguo cha kitambaa
	(*ngoo*-oh chah kee-tah-mb*ah*)
clothes	nguo (*ngoo*-oh)
cloud	wingu (*wee*-ngoo)
club	kilabu (kee-*lah*-boo)
coast	pwani (*pwah*-nee)
coat	koti (*koh*-tee)

cocktail	kinywaji (kee-*nywah*-jee)
coffee	kahawa (kah-*hah*-wah)
cognac	kokna (*kohk*-nah)
cold	baridi (bah-*ree*-dee)
college	chuo (*choo*-oh)
color	rangi (*rah*-ngee)
Colombian	Mkolombia (mkoh-loh-*mbee*-ah)
comb	kichanuo (kee-chah-*noo*-oh)
come	njoo, kuja (njoo), (*koo*-jah)
come in	karibu, ingia (kah-*ree*-boo), (ee-*ngee*-ah)
come here	njoo hapa (njoo *hah*-pah)
comfortable	cha kuburudisha (chah koo-boo-roo-*dee*-shah)
common	cha kawaida (chah kah-wah-*ee*-dah)
communist	komunisti (koh-moo-*nee*-stee)
company	kambi (*kah*-mbee)
comparison	ulinganishi (oo-lee-ngah-*nee*-shee)
compliment	sifu (*see*-foo)
conceited	-enye majivuno (*eh*-nyeh mah-jee-*voo*-noh)
concert	onyesho (oh-*nyeh*-shoh)
condition	hali (*hah*-lee)
confused	-enye wasiwasi (*eh*-nyeh *wah*-see-*wah*-see)
congratulations	shangilia (shah-ngee-*lee*-ah)
congress	mkutano (mkoo-*tah*-noh)
consider	kufikiria (koo-fee-kee-*ree*-ah)
consul	balozi (bah-*loh*-zee)
consulate	nyumba ya balozi (*nyoo*-mbah yah bah-*loh*-zee)
contain	kuchukua (koo-choo-*koo*-ah)
contented	ridhikiwa (ree-thee-*kee*-wah)
continent	bara (*bah*-rah)
continue	endelea (eh-ndeh-*leh*-ah)
convenient	ya kufaa (yah koo-*fah*)
cook	mpishi (*mpee*-shee)

copy	nakili, fuatisha (nah-*kee*-lee), (foo-ah-tee-shah)
corn	mahindi (mah-*hee*-ndee)
corner	pembe (*peh*-mbeh)
correct	sawasisha (sah-wah-*see*-shah)
cost	gharama (ghah-*rah*-mah)
cotton	pamba (*pah*-mbah)
count	hesabu (heh-*sah*-boo)
country	nchi (*n*-chee)
court	kortini (kohr-*tee*-nee)
cow	ng'ombe (ng'*oh*-mbeh)
crazy	mwenye wazimu (*mweh*-nyeh wah-*zee*-moo)
cross	msalaba (msah-*lah*-bah)
crowd	kundi (*koo*-ndee)
cry	lia (*lee*-ah)
crystal	jiwe la kung'ara (*jee*-weh lah koo-ng'*ah*-rah)
cup	kikombe (kee-*koh*-mbeh)
curve	kizingo (kee-*zee*-ngoh)
cut	kata (*kah*-tah)
damaged	haribu (hah-*ree*-boo)
damp	majimaji (*mah*-jee-*mah*-jee)
dance	cheza ngoma (*cheh*-zah *ngoh*-mah)
dangerous	ya hatari (yah hah-*tah*-ree)
dark	giza (*gee*-zah)
date	tarehe (tah-*reh*-heh)
day	siku (*see*-koo)
dead	mfu (*m*foo)
dear	mpenzi (*m*peh-nzee)
December	Desemba (Deh-*seh*-mbah)
deck	pamba, vika vizuri (pah-mbah), (*vee*-kah vee-*zoo*-ree)
deep	kimo (*kee*-moh)
deer	kalungu (kah-*loo*-ngoo)
delay	chelewesha (cheh-leh-*weh*-shah)
delighted	furahishwa (foo-rah-*hee*-shwah)

deliver	peleka (peh-*leh*-kah)
democracy	demokrasi (deh-moh-*krah*-see)
dentist	daktari wa meno (dahk-*tah*-ree wah *meh*-noh)
departure	kutoka (koo-*toh*-kah)
deposit	akiba (ah-*kee*-bah)
descend	shuka(*shoo*-kah)
describe	eleza (eh-*leh*-zah)
desert	jangwa (*jah*-ngwah)
deserve	stahili (stah-*hee*-lee)
desire	tamani (tah-*mah*-nee)
dessert	maandazi (mah-ah-*ndah*-zee)
develop	sitawisha (see-tah-*wee*-shah)
diamond	almasi (ahl-*mah*-see)
dictation	imla (*ee*-mlah)
difference	tofauti (toh-fah-*oo*-tee)
different	tofauti (toh-fah-*oo*-tee)
difficult	ngumu (*ngoo*-moo)
dining room	chumba cha kulia (*choo*-mbah chah koo-*lee*-ah)
dinner	chakula cha kutwa (chah-*koo*-lah chah *koo*-twah)
direct	ongoza kwa kueleza (oh-*ngoh*-zah kwah koo-eh-*leh*-zah)
direction	maelezo ya amri (mah-eh-*leh*-zoh yah *ah*-mree)
director	mtoa amri (*mtoh*-ah *ah*-mree)
dirty	chafu (*chah*-foo)
disadvantage	mazuio (mah-zoo-*ee*-oh)
disappeared	toweka (toh-*weh*-kah)
discount	tohesabu (toh-heh-*sah*-boo)
disease	radhi (*rah*-thee)
dish	sahani (sah-*hah*-nee)
disinfect	safisha (sah-*fee*-shah)
dismiss	fukuza (foo-*koo*-zah)
distance	umbali (oo-*mbah*-lee)
district	jimbo (*jee*-mboh)
disturb	vuruga (voo-*roo*-gah)

divorced	talaka (tah-*lah*-kah)
do	fanya (*fah*-nyah)
dock	gudi (*goo*-dee)
doctor	mganga (*mgah*-ngah)
dog	mbwa (mbw*ah*)
doll	mwanasere (mwah-nah-*seh*-reh)
dollar	dola (*doh*-lah)
domestic	ya nyumbani (yah *nyoo*-mbah-nee)
done	fanywa (*fah*-nywah)
donkey	punda (*poo*-ndah)
door	mlango (*mlah*-ngoh)
dose	kiasi ya dawa (kee-*ah*-see yah *dah*-wah)
double	maradufu (mah-rah-*doo*-foo)
down	chini (*chee*-nee)
dozen	kumi na mbili (*koo*-mee nah *mbee*-lee)
draft	kielezo (kee-eh-*leh*-zoh)
drawer	mtoaji (mtoh-*ah*-jee)
dress	rinda (*ree*-ndah)
dressmaker	mshonaji (mshoh-*nah*-jee)
drink (*to*)	kunywa (*koo*-nywah)
drive (*to*)	kuendesha (koo-eh-*ndeh*-shah)
driver	dereva (deh-*reh*-vah)
drugstore	duka ya dawa (*doo*-kah yah *dah*-wah)
drunk	lewa (*leh*-wah)
dry	kavu (*kah*-voo)
duck	bata (*bah*-tah)
dust	vumbi (*voo*-mbee)
dye	tia rangi (*tee*-ah *rah*-ngee)
each	kila moja (*kee*-lah *moh*-jah)
ear	sikio (see-*kee*-oh)
early	mapema (mah-*peh*-mah)
earn	chuma (*choo*-mah)
earth	ulimwengu (oo-lee-*mweh*-ngoo)
east	mashariki (mah-shah-*ree*-kee)

easy	rahisi (rah-*hee*-see)
eat (*to*)	kula (*koo*-lah)
edge	kando (*kah*-ndoh)
education	maarifa (mah-ah-*ree*-fah)
egg	yai (*yah*-ee)
elastic	ya kuvutika (yah koo-voo-*tee*-kah)
elbow	kumbo (*koo*-mboh)
electric	ya stimu (yah *stee*-moo)
elevator	mtambo wa kuinua (*mtah*-mboh wah koo-ee-*noo*-ah)
embarrassed	kuona haya (koo-*oh*-nah *hah*-yah)
embrace	mbatia (mbah-*tee*-ah)
embroidery	pambo (*pah*-mboh)
emerald	zumaradi (zoo-mah-*rah*-dee)
emergency	hali ya hatari (*hah*-lee yah hah-*tah*-ree)
empty	tupu (*too*-poo)
encore	tena (*teh*-nah)
end	mwisho (*mwee*-shoh)
engaged	poswa (*poh*-swah)
English	Kiingereza (kee-ee-ngeh-*reh*-zah)
enough	yatosha (yah-*toh*-shah)
enter	ingia (ee-*ngee*-ah)
envelope	bahasha (bah-*hah*-shah)
Episcopal	ya askofu (yah-ah-*sko*-foo)
equal	sawa (*sah*-wah)
equipment	vyombo (*vyoh*-mboh)
error	kosa (*koh*-sah)
estate	shamba (*shah*-mbah)
European	mzungu (*mzoo*-ngoo)
evening	jioni (jee-*oh*-nee)
every	kila (*kee*-lah)
evidently	dhahiri (thah-*hee*-ree)
exact	kamili (kah-*mee*-lee)
examination	mtihani (mtee-*hah*-nee)
example	mfano (*mfah*-noh)
except	ila (*ee*-lah)
exchange	badilisho (bah-dee-*lee*-shoh)

excursion	matembezi (mah-teh-*mbeh*-zee)
excuse	udhuru (oo-*thoo*-roo)
excuse me	niwie radhi (nee-*wee*-eh *rah*-thee)
exit	njia ya kutoka (*njee*-ah yah koo-*toh*-kah)
expect	tumaini (too-mah-*ee*-nee)
expensive	ghali (*ghah*-lee)
explain	eleza (eh-*leh*-zah)
express	haraka (hah-*rah*-kah)
extra	zaidi (zah-*ee*-dee)
eye	jicho (*jee*-choh)
face	uso (*oo*-soh)
factory	mtambo (*mtah*-mboh)
fade	toweka (toh-*weh*-kah)
fall	anguka (ah-*ngoo*-kah)
false	uwongo (oo-*woh*-ngoh)
family	jamii (jah-m*ee*)
fan	rafiki (rah-*fee*-kee)
far	mbali (*mbah*-lee)
fare	nauli (nah-*oo*-lee)
farm	shamba (*shah*-mbah)
fashion	mtindo (*mtee*-ndoh)
fast	upesi (oo-*peh*-see)
fat	nene (*neh*-neh)
father	baba (*bah*-bah)
fault	kosa (*koh*-sah)
favor	kuonelea (koo-oh-neh-*leh*-ah)
feather	unyoya (oo-*nyoh*-yah)
feel	sikia mwilini (see-*kee*-ah mwee-*lee*-nee)
female	wa kike (wah *kee*-keh)
fence	ua (*oo*-ah)
fender	kizuizi (kee-zoo-*ee*-zee)
fever	homa (*hoh*-mah)
few	chache (*chah*-cheh)
fight	pigana (pee-*gah*-nah)
fill	jaza (*jah*-zah)

final	ya mwisho (yah *mwee*-shoh)
finger	kidole (kee-*doh*-leh)
finish	maliza (mah-*lee*-zah)
fire	moto (*moh*-toh)
fish	samaki (sah-*mah*-kee)
fit	tosha (*toh*-shah)
fix	tengeneza (teh-ngeh-*neh*-zah)
flag	bendera (beh-*ndeh*-rah)
flat	ubapa (oo-*bah*-pah)
flight	ukimbizi (oo-kee-*mbee*-zee)
flood	gharika (ghah-*ree*-kah)
floor	sakafu (sah-*kah*-foo)
flower	ua (*oo*-ah)
fly (to)	rukia (roo-*kee*-ah)
follow (to)	fuata (foo-*ah*-tah)
food	chakula (chah-*koo*-lah)
foot	guu (goo)
forbid	zuia (zoo-*ee*-ah)
foreigner	mgeni (*mgeh*-nee)
forget (to)	sahau (sah-*hah*-oo)
forgive (to)	samehe (sah-*meh*-heh)
fork	uma (*oo*-mah)
fort	komba (*koh*-mbah)
fountain	kizima (kee-*zee*-mah)
fragile	mbovu (*mboh*-voo)
freedom	uhuru (oo-*hoo*-roo)
freight	shehena (sheh-*heh*-nah)
French	Kifaransa (kee-fah-*rah*-nsah)
frequently	mara kwa mara (*mah*-rah kwah *mah*-rah)
fresh	bichi (*bee*-chee)
fried	iliyokaangwa (ee-lee-yoh-kah-*ah*-ngwah)
friend	rafiki (rah-*fee*-kee)
frozen	imeganda (ee-meh-*gah*-ndah)
fruit	matunda (mah-*too*-ndah)
full	jazwa (*jah*-zwah)
funeral	maziko (mah-*zee*-koh)

funny	ya kuchekesha (yah koo-cheh-*keh*-shah)
further	mbali zaidi (*mbah*-lee zah-*ee*-dee)
future	ijayo (ee-*jah*-yoh)
gain	faida (fah-*ee*-dah)
gallon	galani (gah-*lah*-nee)
gamble	cheza kamari (*cheh*-zah kah-*mah*-ree)
game	mchezo (*mcheh*-zoh)
garbage	ghasia (ghah-*see*-ah)
garden	shamba (*shah*-mbah)
generous	mkarimu (mkah-*ree*-moo)
geography	jographia (joh-grah-*phee*-ah)
German	Mdachi (*mdah*-chee)
get (*to*)	kupata (koo-*pah*-tah)
gift	zawadi (zah-*wah*-dee)
girl	msichana (msee-*chah*-nah)
glass	kioo (kee-oh)
go (*to*)	kwenda (*kweh*-ndah)
God	Mungu (*moo*-ngoo)
goodbye	kwa heri (kwah *heh*-ree)
government	serikali (seh-ree-*kah*-lee)
grass	majani (mah-*jah*-nee)
grateful	mshukuru (mshoo-*koo*-roo)
grease	mafuta (mah-*foo*-tah)
grow (*to*)	kumea (koo-*meh*-ah)
guest	mgeni (*mgeh*-nee)
guide	mwongozi (mwoh-*ngoh*-zee)
gun	bunduki (boo-*ndoo*-kee)
hair	nywele (*nyweh*-leh)
half	nusu (*noo*-soo)
halt!	simamisha (see-mah-*mee*-shah)
hammer	nyundo (*nyoo*-ndoh)
hand	mkono (*mkoh*-noh)
happen (*to*)	kutokea (koo-toh-*keh*-ah)

happy	furahi (foo-*rah*-hee)
harbor	bandari (bah-*ndah*-ree)
hard	vigumu (vee-*goo*-moo)
hat	kofia (koh-*fee*-ah)
hate (*to*)	kuchukia (koo-choo-*kee*-ah)
have (*to*)	kuwa na (*koo*-wah nah)
head	kichwa (*kee*-chwah)
health	hali ya mwili (*hah*-lee yah *mwee*-lee)
hear (*to*)	kusikia (koo-see-*kee*-ah)
heat	joto (*joh*-toh)
heavy	zito (*zee*-toh)
hell	ahera (ah-*heh*-rah)
help (*to*)	kusaidia (koo-sah-ee-*dee*-ah)
here	hapa (*hah*-pah)
high	juu (*joo*)
hill	mlima (*mlee*-mah)
history	historia (hee-stoh-*ree*-ah)
hit (*to*)	kupiga (koo-*pee*-gah)
hole	shimo (*shee*-moh)
holiday	ruhusa (roo-*hoo*-sah)
holy	takatifu (tah-kah-*tee*-foo)
honest	aminifu (ah-mee-*nee*-foo)
honor	heshimu (heh-*shee*-moo)
horse	farasi (fah-*rah*-see)
hour	saa (s*ah*)
human	kibinadamu (kee-bee-nah-*dah*-moo)
hunger	njaa (nj*ah*)
hunting	kuwinda (koo-*wee*-ndah)
hurricane	tifani (tee-*fah*-nee)
hurt (*to*)	umiza (oo-*mee*-zah)
	mimi (*mee*-mee)
ice	theluji (theh-*loo*-jee)
identification	utambulizi (oo-tah-mboo-*lee*-zee)
ignorant	pumbavu (poo-*mbah*-voo)
ill	gonjwa (*goh*-njwah)
illegal	haramu (hah-*rah*-moo)
illustration	michoro (mee-*choh*-roh)

imitation	uigaji (oo-ee-*gah*-jee)
immediate	mara moja (*mah*-rah *moh*-jah)
important	ya maana (yah mah-*ah*-nah)
impossible	isiyowezekana (*ee*-see-yoh-weh-zeh-*kah*-nah)
inch	ichi (*ee*-nchee)
included	imeungwa (ee-meh-*oo*-ngwah)
incorrect	isiyo sawa (ee-*see*-yoh *sah*-wah)
increase	ongeza (oh-*ngeh*-zah)
independence	isiyotegemea (ee-see-yoh-teh-geh-*meh*-ah)
indigestion	tumbo ya kuuma (*too*-mboh yah koo-*oo*-mah)
indoors	ya nyumbani (yah nyoo-*mbah*-nee)
infection	ambukizo (ah-mboo-*kee*-zoh)
informal	siyo taratibu (*see*-yoh tah-rah-*tee*-boo)
injection	tia sindano (*tee*-ah see-*ndah*-noh)
injury	umivu (oo-*mee*-voo)
ink	wino (*wee*-noh)
innocent	bila hatia (*bee*-lah hah-*tee*-ah)
insane	mwenye wazimu (*mweh*-nyeh wah-*zee*-moo)
inspect (to)	kukagua (koo-kah-*goo*-ah)
institution	chuo (*choo*-oh)
intelligent	mwenye akili (*mweh*-nyeh ah-*kee*-lee)
interesting	wa kufurahisha (wah koo-foo-rah-*hee*-shah)
international	ya ulimwengu (yah oo-lee-*mweh*-ngoo)
interpret (to)	kutafsiri (koo-tahf-*see*-ree)
introduce (to)	kujulisha (koo-joo-*lee*-shah)
investigate (to)	kupeleleza (koo-peh-leh-*leh*-zah)
invite (to)	kualika (koo-ah-*lee*-kah)
iron	chuma (*choo*-mah)
island	kisiwa (kee-*see*-wah)
ivory	pembe ndovu (*peh*-mbeh *ndoh*-voo)

jail	jela (*jeh*-lah)
Japanese	Kijapani (kee-jah-*pah*-nee)
jaw	taya (*tah*-yah)
job	kazi (*kah*-zee)
joke	mzaha (*mzah*-hah)
judge	wakili (wah-*kee*-lee)
juice	utomvu (oo-*toh*-mvoo)
jungle	msitu (*msee*-too)
justice	sheria (sheh-*ree*-ah)
key	ufunguo (oo-foo-*ngoo*-oh)
kill (*to*)	kuwa (*koo*-wah)
king	mfalme (*mfahl*-meh)
kiss	busu (*boo*-soo)
kitchen	jiko (*jee*-koh)
knife	kisu (*kee*-soo)
knock (*to*)	kugonga (koo-*goh*-ngah)
know (*to*)	kujua (koo-*joo*-ah)
lake	ziwa (*zee*-wah)
lame	kiwete (kee-*weh*-teh)
lamp	taa (*tah*)
language	lugha (*loo*-ghah)
late	chelewa (cheh-*leh*-wah)
law	sheria (sheh-*ree*-ah)
lazy	legevi (leh-*geh*-vee)
leaf	jani (*jah*-nee)
learn (*to*)	kujifunza (koo-jee-*foo*-nzah)
leather	ngozi (*ngoh*-zee)
leg	mguu (m*goo*)
letter	baruwa (bah-*roo*-wah)
license	leseni (leh-*seh*-nee)
lie	uwongo (oo-*woh*-ngoh)
life	maisha (mah-*ee*-shah)
lip	domo (*doh*-moh)
lion	simba (*see*-mbah)
locomotive	gari (*gah*-ree)
look (*to*)	kutazama (koo-tah-*zah*-mah)

lose (*to*)	kupoteza (koo-poh-*teh*-zah)
loud	sauti ya juu (sah-*oo*-tee yah joo)
love	upendo (oo-*peh*-ndoh)
low	ya chini (yah *chee*-nee)
luck	hahati (bah-*hah*-tee)
lunch	chakula cha mchana (chah-*koo*-lah chah *mchah*-nah)
machine	mashine (mah-*shee*-neh)
mail	posta (*poh*-stah)
man	mtu (*m*-too)
many	wengi (*weh*-ngee)
map	ramani (rah-*mah*-nee)
market	soko (*soh*-koh)
marry (*to*)	kuoa (koo-*oh*-ah)
massage	utume (oo-*too*-meh)
match	kiberiti (kee-beh-*ree*-tee)
meal	chakula (chah-*koo*-lah)
measure	pima (*pee*-mah)
meat	nyama (*nyah*-mah)
medicine	dawa (*dah*-wah)
memory	ukumbusho (oo-koo-*mboo*-shoh)
message	taarifa (tah-ah-*ree*-fah)
mile	mailo (mah-*ee*-loh)
military	kiaskari (kee-ah-*skah*-ree)
minute	dakika (dah-*kee*-kah)
mistake	kosa (*koh*-sah)
modern	ya kisasa (yah kee-*sah*-sah)
money	pesa (*peh*-sah)
monkey	tumbili (too-*mbee*-lee)
moon	mwezi (*mweh*-zee)
morning	asubuhi (ah-soo-*boo*-hee)
mosquito	mbu (*mboo*)
mother	mama (*mah*-mah)
mouth	mdomo (*mdoh*-moh)
move (*to*)	kusongea (koo-soh-*ngeh*-ah)
Mr.	Bwana (*bwah*-nah)
Mrs.	Bibi (*bee*-bee)

mud	tope (*toh*-peh)
mule	nyumbu (*nyoo*-mboo)
murder	uuwaji (oo-oo-*wah*-jee)
music	wimbo (*wee*-mboh)
naked	uchi (*oo*-chee)
narrow	bamba (*bah*-mbah)
nation	taifa (tah-*ee*-fah)
navy	uanamaji (oo-ah-nah-*mah*-jee)
necessary	ya muhimu (yah moo-*hee*-moo)
neck	shingo (*shee*-ngoh)
need (*to*)	kutaka (koo-*tah*-kah)
Negro	Mweusi (mweh-*oo*-see)
nerve	neva (*neh*-vah)
never	kamwe (*kah*-mweh)
new	mpya (mpy*ah*)
night	usiku (oo-*see*-koo)
no	la (lah)
nose	pua (*poo*-ah)
nothing	si kitu (see *kee*-too)
now	sasa (*sah*-sah)
nurse	mlezi (*mleh*-zee)
obvious	wazi (*wah*-zee)
occupied	imeshikwa (ee-meh-*shee*-kwah)
ocean	bahari (bah-*hah*-ree)
odd	si kamili (see kah-*mee*-lee)
odor	nuko (*noo*-koh)
office	afisi (ah-*fee*-see)
old	zee (zee)
operation	matendo (mah-*teh*-ndoh)
opinion	nia (*nee*-ah)
opportunity	nafasi (nah-*fah*-see)
order (*to*)	kuamuru (koo-ah-*moo*-roo)
oriental	ya kishariki (yah kee-shah-*ree*-kee)
orphan	yatima (yah-*tee*-mah)
ounce	wakia (wah-*kee*-ah)
our	yetu (*yeh*-too)

oven	jiko (jee-*koh*)
owner	mwenye (*mweh*-nyeh)
oyster	chaza (*chah*-zah)
pack (*to*)	kufunga safari (koo-*foo*-ngah sah-*fah*-ree)
page	ukarasa (oo-kah-*rah*-sah)
paid	imelipwa (ee-meh-*lee*-pwah)
pain	uchungu (oo-*choo*-ngoo)
painting	machoro (mah-*choh*-roh)
palm	mnazi (*mnah*-zee)
paralyzed	poozesha (poh-oh-*zeh*-shah)
park	bustani (boo-*stah*-nee)
party	karamu (kah-*rah*-moo)
passenger	abiria (ah-bee-*ree*-ah)
peace	amani (ah-*mah*-nee)
pen	kalamu (kah-*lah*-moo)
pencil	kalamu ya mate (kah-*lah*-moo yah *mah*-teh)
penalty	adhabu (ah-*thah*-boo)
people	watu (*wah*-too)
perfect	kamili (kah-*mee*-lee)
permit (*to*)	kuruhusu (koo-roo-*hoo*-soo)
photograph	picha (*pee*-chah)
pillow	mto (*m*toh)
pilot	rubani (roo-*bah*-nee)
pipe	kiko (*kee*-koh)
pistol	bastola (bah-*stoh*-lah)
planet	sayari (sah-*yah*-ree)
pleasure	furaha (foo-*rah*-hah)
pocket	mfuko (*mfoo*-koh)
poisonous	ya sumu (yah *soo*-moo)
police	polisi (poh-*lee*-see)
political	ya utetezi (yah oo-teh-*teh*-zee)
poor	maskini (mah-*skee*-nee)
popular	cha kupendwa (chah koo-*peh*-ndwah)
pound	pauni (pah-*oo*-nee)
power	nguvu (*ngoo*-voo)

premier	waziri mkuu (wah-*zee*-ree mk*oo*)
prepare (*to*)	kutayarisha (koo-tah-yah-*ree*-shah)
price	bei (*beh*-ee)
priest	askofu (ah-*skoh*-foo)
prison	korkoroni (kohr-koh-*roh*-nee)
private	ya pekee (yah peh-k*e*h)
professor	mwalimu (mwah-*lee*-moo)
profit	faida (fah-*ee*-dah)
proof	thibitisho (thee-bee-*tee*-shoh)
propaganda	maenezi (mah-eh-*neh*-zee)
prosperity	faniki (fah-*nee*-kee)
province	jimbo (*jee*-mboh)
public	ya raia (yah rah-*ee*-ah)
pure	safi (*sah*-fee)
quality	aina (ah-*ee*-nah)
question	swali (*swah*-lee)
quick	upesi (oo-*peh*-see)
quiet	pasipo kelele (pah-*see*-poh keh-*leh*-leh)
radio	simu ya upepo (*see*-moo yah oo-*peh*-poh)
railroad	reli ya gari (*reh*-lee yah *gah*-ree)
rain	mvua (*mvoo*-ah)
raw	bichi (*bee*-chee)
razor blade	wembe (*weh*-mbeh)
reach (*to*)	kufikia (koo-fee-*kee*-ah)
read (*to*)	kusoma (koo-*soh*-mah)
rear	nyuma (*nyoo*-mah)
receive	pata (*pah*-tah)
recommend (*to*)	kusifu (koo-*see*-foo)
refund (*to*)	kulipa (koo-*lee*-pah)
relative	jamaa (jah-*mah*)
religion	dini (*dee*-nee)
remember (*to*)	kukumbuka (koo-koo-*mboo*-kah)
repair (*to*)	kutengeneza (koo-teh-ngeh-*neh*-zah)
reply	jibu

represent (*to*)	kutetea (koo-teh-*teh*-ah)
respect	heshimu (heh-*shee*-moo)
rest (*to*)	kupumzika (koo-poo-*mzee*-kah)
return (*to*)	kurudi (koo-*roo*-dee)
revolution	uasi (oo-*ah*-see)
rice	mchele (*mcheh*-leh)
rich	tajiri (tah-*jee*-ree)
ride	panda (*pah*-ndah)
river	mto (*m*toh)
road	njia (*njee*-ah)
roast	choma (*choh*-mah)
romantic	ya ajabu (yah-ah-*jah*-boo)
roof	paa (p*ah*)
room	chumba (*choo*-mbah)
rope	kamba (*kah*-mbah)
round	viringo (vee-*ree*-ngoh)
rubber	mpira (*mpee*-rah)
Russia	Urusi (oo-*roo*-see)
saddle	upando (oo-*pah*-ndoh)
salt	chumvi (*choo*-mvee)
sand	mchanga (*mchah*-ngah)
satisfactory	ya kutosha (yah koo-*toh*-shah)
save (*to*)	koukoa (koo-oh-*koh*-ah)
scarf	sikafu (see-*kah*-foo)
schedule	taarifa (tah-ah-*ree*-fah)
school	shule (*shoo*-leh)
science	utaalamu (oo-tah-ah-*lah*-moo)
scratch	kwaruza (kwah-*roo*-zah)
see (*to*)	kuona (koo-*oh*-nah)
sell (*to*)	kuuza (koo-*oo*-zah)
separate (*to*)	kutenga (koo-*teh*-ngah)
service	kazi (*kah*-zee)
sew (*to*)	kushona (koo-*shoh*-nah)
shave (*to*)	kunyoa (koo-*nyoh*-ah)
sheep	kondoo (koh-ndoh)
ship	merikebu (meh-ree-*keh*-boo)
shoe	kiatu (kee-*ah*-too)

shower (*bath*)	kioga (kee-*oh*-gah)
sick	gonjwa (*goh*-njwah)
sign	alama (ah-*lah*-mah)
sing (*to*)	kuimba (koo-*ee*-mbah)
sister	dada (*dah*-dah)
sit (*to*)	kukaa (koo-k*ah*)
skin	ngozi (*ngoh*-zee)
sky	anga (*ah*-ngah)
sleep (*to*)	kulala (koo-*lah*-lah)
slippery	ya kuteleza (yah koo-teh-*leh*-zah)
slow	pole (*poh*-leh)
smell	nuka (*noo*-kah)
smile	cheka (*cheh*-kah)
smoke (*to*)	kuvuta sigara (koo-*voo*-tah see-*gah*-rah)
snake	nyoka (*nyoh*-kah)
soap	sabuni (sah-*boo*-nee)
soft	nyororo (nyoh-*roh*-roh)
son	mwana (*mwah*-nah)
sorry	pole (*poh*-leh)
sound	sauti (sah-*oo*-tee)
sour	chungu (*choo*-ngoo)
Spanish	Kispaniola (kee-spah-nee-*oh*-lah)
speak (*to*)	kusema (koo-*seh*-mah)
spider	buibui (boo-ee-*boo*-ee)
spoon	kijiko (kee-*jee*-koh)
square	mraba (*mrah*-bah)
stairs	ngazi ya dari (*ngah*-zee yah *dah*-ree)
station	stesheni (steh-*sheh*-nee)
steel	chuma cha pua (*choo*-mah chah *poo*-ah)
sting	uma (*oo*-mah)
stomach	tumbo (*too*-mboh)
straight	nyoroka (nyoh-*roh*-kah)
straw	majani makavu (mah-*jah*-nee mah-*kah*-voo)
street	njia ya mjini (*njee*-ah yah *mjee*-nee)
success	ushindi (oo-*shee*-ndee)

sugar	sukari (soo-*kah*-ree)
suit	suti (*soo*-tee)
sweep (*to*)	kufagia (koo-fah-*gee*-ah)
sweet	tamu (*tah*-moo)
swim (*to*)	kuogelea (koo-oh-geh-*leh*-ah)
table	meza (*meh*-zah)
tail	mkia (*mkee*-ah)
tall	ndefu (*ndeh*-foo)
teach (*to*)	kufundisha (koo-foo-*ndee*-shah)
terrible	ya kutisha (yah koo-*tee*-shah)
test	jaribu (jah-*ree*-boo)
theater	sinema (see-*neh*-mah)
then	ndipo (*ndee*-poh)
thick	nene (*neh*-neh)
thief	mwivi (*mwee*-vee)
thin	konda (*koh*-ndah)
think (*to*)	kufikiri (koo-fee-*kee*-ree)
thirsty	kiu (*kee*-oo)
throw (*to*)	kutupa (koo-*too*-pah)
ticket	cheti (*cheh*-tee)
tired	choka (*choh*-kah)
toilet	ya kuoga (yah koo-*oh*-gah)
torn	raruka (rah-*roo*-kah)
towel	taulo (tah-*oo*-loh)
travel (*to*)	kutembea (koo-teh-*mbeh*-ah)
tree	mti (*m*tee)
trouble	matata (mah-*tah*-tah)
truck	lori (*loh*-ree)
true	kweli (*kweh*-lee)
turn (*to*)	kugeuka (koo-geh-*oo*-kah)
typewriter	tapureta (tah-poo-*reh*-tah)
umbrella	mwavuli (mwah-*voo*-lee)
understand (*to*)	kufahamu (koo-fah-*hah*-moo)
undress (*to*)	kutoa nguo (koo-*toh*-ah *ngoo*-oh)
unfair	si halali (see hah-*lah*-lee)
uniform	sawasisha (sah-wah-*see*-shah)

union	umoja (oo-*moh*-jah)
United States	Amerika (ah-meh-*ree*-kah)
university	chuo (*choo*-oh)
until	mpaka (*mpah*-kah)
useful	ya faida (yah fah-*ee*-dah)
useless	ya bure (yah *boo*-reh)
valuable	ya thamani (yah thah-*mah*-nee)
vegetables	mboga (*mboh*-gah)
view	upeo wa macho (oo-*peh*-oh wah *mah*-choh)
visit (to)	kutembelea (koo-teh-mbeh-*leh*-ah)
wait (to)	kungoja (koo-*ngoh*-jah)
walk (to)	kutembea (koo-teh-*mbeh*-ah)
wall	ukuta (oo-*koo*-tah)
wash (to)	kusafisha (koo-sah-*fee*-shah)
watch (to)	kuchunga (koo-*choo*-ngah)
water	maji (*mah*-jee)
weak	dhaifu (thah-*ee*-foo)
wear (to)	kuvaa (koo-v*ah*)
weather	hali ya hewa (*hah*-lee yah *heh*-wah)
weigh (to)	kupima (koo-*pee*-mah)
wet	majimaji (mah-jee-*mah*-jee)
wheel	gurudumu (goo-roo-*doo*-moo)
when	lini (*lee*-nee)
where	wapi (*wah*-pee)
wide	pana (*pah*-nah)
wild	ya mwituni (yah mwee-*too*-nee)
win (to)	kushinda (koo-*shee*-ndah)
wind	upepo (oo-*peh*-poh)
wine	divai (dee-*vah*-ee)
window	dirisha (dee-*ree*-shah)
wisdom	busara (boo-*sah*-rah)
wish	matakwa (mah-*tah*-kwah)
without	bila (*bee*-lah)
woman	mwanamke (mwah-*nah*-mkeh)
wood	ubao (oo-*bah*-oh)

work (*to*)	kufanya kazi (koo-*fah*-nyah *kah*-zee)
world	dunia (doo-*nee*-ah)
wrist	kiwiko (kee-*wee*-koh)
write (*to*)	kuandika (koo-ah-*ndee*-kah)
year	mwaka (*mwah*-kah)
young	changa (*chah*-ngah)
zebra	twiga (*twee*-gah)
zoo	zoo (zoh)

METRIC MEASURE

1 centimeter	= .3937 inch
1 meter	= 39.37 inches
1 kilometer	= .62137 mile
1 kilogram	= 2.2046 pounds
1 liter	= 1.0567 quarts (liquid)
1 inch	= 2.54 centimeters
1 foot	= .3048 meter
1 yard	= .9144 meter
1 mile	= 1.6093 kilometers
1 pound	= .4536 kilogram
1 quart	= .9463 liter (liquid)

CURRENCY

Angola	*Escudo*	.042
Botswana	*Rand*	1.480
Republic of Burundi	*Franc*	.006
Zaire	*Zaire*	.085
Ethiopia	*Dollar*	.150
Kenya	*Shilling*	.100
Malawi	*Pound*	.400
Mozambique	*Escudo*	.035
Rhodesia	*Pound*	1.00
Rwanda	*Franc*	.006
South Africa (Republic)	*Rand*	1.20
Tanzania	*Shilling*	.050
Uganda	*Shilling*	.050
Zambia	*Kwacha*	.500

Owing to fluctuations in the exchange rate all quotations above should be considered only as general guidelines. Before any trip check with your bank.